BORDERS AND BELONGING

BORDERS AND BELONGING

TOWARD A FAIR IMMIGRATION POLICY

HIROSHI MOTOMURA

OXFORD
UNIVERSITY PRESS

Oxford University Press is a department of the University of Oxford.
It furthers the University's objective of excellence in research, scholarship,
and education by publishing worldwide. Oxford is a registered trade mark of
Oxford University Press in the UK and in certain other countries.

Published in the United States of America by Oxford University Press
198 Madison Avenue, New York, NY 10016, United States of America.

CIP data is on file at the Library of Congress

ISBN 9780197743720

DOI: 10.1093/oso/9780197743720.001.0001

Printed by Integrated Books International, United States of America

Cover image: the author and his mother leaving for America and bidding farewell to her parents,
Port of Yokohama, Japan, 1957.

For Mari and Naomi

Contents

Acknowledgments   x

Introduction   1
   Writing About Borders   2
   Key Themes and Disruptive Ideas   3
   A Few Disclaimers   5
   A Roadmap   7
   Two Approaches in Tension   8

PART I BORDERS AND CLAIMS

1. **Why National Borders, and Why Not?**   15
   Boundaries in Other Settings   16
   Moving Toward Better Borders   18
   Humanity Claims   19
   Belonging Claims   20
   Integration and Belonging   21

2. **What Are Better Responses to Forced Migration?**   23
   Refugee Protection Since World War II   24
   Protection Under Stress   27
   Managing and Limiting Protection   28
   Approaches to Protection   32
   Finding Better Responses   37

3. **Who Can Say That They Belong?**   41
   Race in Immigration History   42

Turning to Civil Rights   46
Defining Insiders   50
The Interests of Insiders   52
The Limits of National Belonging   53

PART II ADMISSION, EXCLUSION, AND TIME

4. **Who Should Get In, or Be Kept Out?**   57
Families   57
Workers and Investors   62
Who Is Kept Out?   65
From Where?   66
Numbers, Integration, and the Undocumented   68

5. **Should Newcomers Stay Temporarily or**
Indefinitely?   70
Temporary Statuses   70
In-between Statuses   72
Reasons for the Temporary and In-between   75
Problems with the Temporary and In-between   78
Choices for Migrants   79

PART III IMMIGRATION OUTSIDE THE LAW
AND ENFORCEMENT

6. **What About People Without Lawful Status?**   85
Labor, Race, and Discretion   86
Legalization in Context   90
Assessing Legalization   93
The Rule of Law   95
The Limits of Legalization   97

7. **What Should Enforcement Do, and Not Do?**   101
Intensifying Immigration Enforcement   102

Enforcement and Discretion   104
Discretion and Discrimination   106
Approaches to Immigration Enforcement   108
Enforcement Reform and Its Limits   115

PART IV DELVING DEEPER

8. **How Can We Take Skeptics Seriously, and Why?**   **119**
Immigration's Economic Effects   120
Immigration's Effects on Public Treasuries   123
Addressing Economic Anxiety   124
Immigration and the Historically Disadvantaged   127
Deeper Anxieties   130

9. **What Does It Mean to Address Migration's Root
   Causes?**   **133**
Making Immigration Policy Alone   134
Addressing Root Causes in Countries of Origin   136
Transit Countries   137
Finding Ways Forward   141
Remittances   143
Transparency and Accountability   145

10. **What's the Big Picture?**   **147**
What Injustices Can National Borders Conceal?   147
How Should Immigration Policy Be Made?   151
How Should History Matter?   156
What Should Immigration Policy Do?   159

Conclusion   **162**

Endnotes   164
Index   189

Acknowledgments

When your acknowledgments cover several pages, you know you've had a lot of help. This book reflects the thought, care, and work of many people and many communities.

I am immensely grateful to many friends and colleagues whose suggestions, comments, questions, and criticisms greatly improved this book. Especially generous with their time and energy by reading the entire manuscript were David Abraham, Silvia Adamo, Alex Aleinikoff, Ahilan Arulanantham, Deep Gulasekaram, Donald Kerwin, Talia Inlender, Charles Kamasaki, Stephen Lee, Matt Lister, David Martin, Marissa Rosenberg-Carlson, and Anna Skarpelis.

I am deeply indebted to the friends and colleagues who not only read the manuscript but also took the time for an all-day workshop on an earlier draft at the Temple University Beasley School of Law in February 2024. They deserve special mention: Lenni Benson, Jacqueline Bhabha, Howard Chang, Muzaffar Chishti, Adam Cox, Alina Das, Alexandra Délano, Jill Family, Jonathan Hafetz, Rebecca Hamlin, Alan Hyde, Anil Kalhan, Elizabeth Keyes, Anna Law, Jennifer Lee, Nancy Morawetz, Jayesh Rathod, Evelyn Rangel-Medina, Peter Spiro, and above all Jaya Ramji-Nogales, who first suggested that we gather.

I also received generous help from many others who participated in workshops, read parts of drafts, and shared their thinking in conversations that shaped what I've written. They include Tendayi Achiume, Diego Acosta Arcarazo, Diane Amann, Sameer Ashar, Elisabeth Badenhoop, Asli Bâli, Mehrsa Baradaran, David Bartram, Jürgen Bast, Rainer Bauböck, Guyora Binder, Irene Bloemraad, Benjamin Boudou, Kathleen Bush-Joseph, Jennifer Chacón, Ming Hsu Chen, Janie Chuang,

Kimberly Clausing, Harlan Grant Cohen, Pooja Dadhania, Derek Denman, Alan Desmond, Ingrid Eagly, Gianna Eckert, Anuscheh Farahat, David FitzGerald, Maryellen Fullerton, Marta Górczyńska, Dieter Gosewinkel, Encarnación Gutiérrez Rodríguez, Michaela Hailbronner, Lisa Harms-Dalibon, Sheila Harrison, Ernesto Hernández-López, Marielena Hincapié, Constantin Hruschka, Rachel Hudson, Kristine Huskey, Peter Jaffey, Arwen Joyce, Jerry Kang, Leila Kawar, Catherine Kim, Sung Hui Kim, Witold Klaus, Jennifer Koh, Ruud Koopmans, Kriszta Kovács, Sarah Krakoff, Mattias Kumm, Dilek Kurban, Annie Lai, Audrey Macklin, Anji Malhotra, David Marcus, Cecilia Menjívar, Katie Meyer, Jon Michaels, Rachel Moran, Jide Nzelibe, Tony O'Rourke, Jason Oh, Greta Olson, Tania Pagotto, K-Sue Park, Marei Pelzer, Margaret Peters, Dario Portong, Nina Rabin, Shalini Bhargava Ray, Mareike Riedel, Carrie Rosenbaum, Bernard Ryan, John Schlegel, Ayelet Shachar, Bijal Shah, André Luiz Siciliano, Anita Sinha, Sarah Song, Alma Stankovic, Kelly Staples, Julia Stier, Juliet Stumpf, Margaret Taylor, Daniel Thym, Martijn van den Brink, Andrew Verstein, Leti Volpp, Frederik von Harbou, Roger Waldinger, Phil Weiser, Janna Wessels, Vanessa Wintermantel, Andrew Woods, and Colin Yeo.

I benefitted greatly from colloquia, workshops, and conferences at the UCLA School of Law, the Immigrants' Rights Policy Clinic and the Immigrant Family Legal Clinic at UCLA Law, the UCLA Center for the Study of International Migration, the American Bar Foundation, the American University Washington College of Law, the Arizona State University Sandra Day O'Connor College of Law, the Association of Asian American Studies Annual Conference, the Bucerius Law School, the Centre of Migration Research in Warsaw, the College of Wooster, the Conference of Asian Pacific American Law Faculty, the DePaul University Migration Collaborative, the Duke University School of Law, the European University Institute, Hamburg University, the Irish Centre for Human Rights at the University of Galway, Justus-Liebig-Universität, the Leicester School of Law at the University of Leicester, the Lewis & Clark Law School, the Loyola Marymount

University Loyola Law School, the Loyola University New Orleans College of Law, the Max Planck Institute for the Study of Religious and Ethnic Diversity, the Migration Policy Institute, the Northwestern Pritzker School of Law, the SMU Dedman School of Law, the Universidad Nacional Autónoma de México, Université Paris II-Panthéon-Assas, the University at Buffalo School of Law, the University of Arizona James E. Rogers College of Law, the University of California, Berkeley, the University of California, Irvine, School of Law, the University of California, San Diego, the University of Connecticut, the University of Copenhagen, the University of Georgia School of Law, the University of Houston Law Center, the University of Minnesota, Twin Cities, the University of Southern California, the University of Warsaw Faculty of Law, the University of Zagreb, the Washington University School of Law, the Western History Association Annual Conference, the Western People of Color Legal Scholar Conference, Western Washington University, the Wissenschaftszentrum Berlin für Sozialforschung, Zhejiang University, and the Zolberg Institute on Migration and Mobility at The New School.

UCLA law students provided excellent research and editorial assistance. I am very grateful to Sarah Fisher, Astghik Hairapetian, Matthew O'Donnell, Addie Black, Henry Cordova, Sophie Kosmacher, Richard Peng, Lucas Beard, Zunaira Sardar, and Robert Rios.

My heartfelt thanks go to Professors Liav Orgad and Ruud Koopmans at the Wissenschaftszentrum Berlin for hosting me for two especially generative semester-long research stays to work on this book.

I completed this manuscript during a four-week residency at the Bellagio Center of the Rockefeller Foundation in Bellagio, Italy. My fellow residents in the May 2024 cohort were a constant source of inspiration and creative energy. In many ways, they prompted me to reimagine the assumptions and approaches that I brought to this book.

This project benefited from generous research funding and support from the John Simon Guggenheim Memorial Foundation, the Rockefeller Foundation, the UCLA School of Law Dean's Discretionary Fund, and the UCLA Academic Senate.

I have attended the Puget Sound Guitar Workshop every summer for twenty-six years (except for two pandemic summers). A very special musical community has shaped my life as a teacher, scholar, and creator, and has profoundly influenced me and this book.

This is my second book with David McBride, my editor at Oxford University Press. I am very grateful for his confidence in this project and for guiding it into being.

Essential to the thinking, research, and writing that have gone into this book has been family: Linda, Amy, Remy, Mari and Naomi, Janna, Gail, Akira, and the memory of our parents.

Some of the thoughts here first took shape while I was engaged in earlier projects, perhaps over my entire career, but this book goes far beyond anything I've published before. Of course, all shortcomings and errors are my own.

Introduction

About This Book

As long as I can remember, borders and belonging have been a big part of my life. My parents brought me from Japan to America at the age of three. I grew up in a working-class immigrant family in San Francisco, constantly struggling to find my place in a country that often welcomes newcomers but also treats many with skepticism and disrespect, and sometimes with hostility.

My journey has reflected my efforts to belong but also to stay true to myself. My predicament was partly economic; my family found it hard to make ends meet. From childhood on, I felt the sting and self-doubt that comes from racial exclusion and stereotyping. But I don't tell you my family history to make my views more legitimate or more worthy of attention. I just want to explain my story in case it might make my views more understandable. My experiences growing up in an immigrant family still strongly influence and inform my thoughts and feelings.

By now I've thought, taught, and written about immigration and citizenship for over thirty years as a professor and much longer as a resident and then a citizen of the United States. With time, I've come to look at the experiences of migrants through a broader lens. I've seen that people of all political persuasions have heartfelt views about newcomers. It's only natural to ask: Who can come in and who can't? Will "they" become "us"?

The answers shape the future. Maybe that's why immigration seems so immediate and personal—for ourselves, our families, and our communities. And maybe that's why it's hard to separate immigration from other public concerns. Attitudes toward immigration often reflect views about equality, race, religion, gender, globalization, government, and much else that can be complex, controversial, and fraught. Discussing immigration leads naturally to imagining and debating what the country or the world should be. Maybe more fundamentally, it leads to questions about how to have that discussion and whose voices should matter. Borders are part of this conversation.

Writing About Borders

If you look at any map of the world, you'll see lines that seem to divide countries from each other. Each country gets its own tint. The lines represent the physical versions of national borders—often in the form of borders and walls. But borders that distinguish countries are much more than the physical borders that divide land on one side from land on the other. Borders don't just mark off areas of land or water. Borders exist in many forms that are less obvious.

Borders also exist in the form of immigration laws that say who may enter, and who may stay or must leave. Other laws say who can—and can't—be citizens. Laws influence whether some people put down roots—or don't settle in the country—by saying who may own land and who may not. Laws regulate participation in politics and access to jobs and social welfare. Some countries have laws that restrict exit. The word "borders" in the title of this book includes all of these sorts of responses to people who try to move from one country to another.

PEOPLE HAVE ALWAYS moved. Migration today continues familiar patterns, even as new contributing factors—such as climate change— emerge over time. To be sure, immigration in many parts of the world plays a more pivotal role than it did at times in the past. And yet it's misleading and dangerous to call the current moment a crisis. This word suggests something unusual, calling for an immediate response, a quick fix.

Another aspect of the word "crisis" is more subtle but more troubling. It can lead to asking only how to make a bad thing better, or how to solve the migration "problem." But it's at least as vital to ask about the ways that migration leads to good. Migration creates opportunities for people, societies, and the world as a whole. It's essential to ask how to make the most of migration as a benefit, not just now but in the future.

All too often, what's said about immigration fails to appreciate the complex choices behind migration and how people and countries might respond to it. Across the political spectrum, many observers speak only to—and hear only from—the like-minded. And though many people ponder tough questions about migration, they often think in insulated political and professional silos that let them avoid hard questions. In this book, I'll try to do better. I'll pose ten questions about migration and explain how they are interwoven. I'll show how the answers to these questions reveal some key themes and offer some disruptive ideas.

Key Themes and Disruptive Ideas

Some key themes emerge from this book. First, national borders can mask injustices by creating zones that dispense with the approaches to fairness and justice that routinely apply inside those borders. The result is often that borders allow injustices to go undetected or unremedied. Some injustices aren't seen as injustices at all. This can happen when dominant elements in a society use borders as a tool to cling to the familiar in the face of change. All too often, the problem is that some voices go unheard while other voices are amplified and dominate.

A second key theme is that it matters a great deal how people and institutions make decisions about immigration. In many chapters, I won't make specific recommendations because the solution to a problem isn't a particular course of action. Rather, the problem is who is missing from the conversation. When governments apply immigration laws and policies to decide the fates of people and communities, it matters who decides, and who influences them. And it's crucial to prevent wrongs, or detect them so they can be remedied.

Third, history should inform immigration policy. Sometimes this broader context can seem immediately relevant and suggest effective responses. Sometimes these contexts can seem too attenuated to persuade decision-makers that history matters. More generally, the broader context reminds us that sustainable responses require thinking over the long term and avoiding quick sugar highs.

Fourth, the dimension of time is crucial. Human migration today reflects decades, generations, or even centuries of past decision-making. Wise and effective responses will take time to make a sustainable difference. Responses should look beyond swift results to take the long view, with the sort of patience that extends beyond immediate election cycles or other short-term thinking.

THIS BOOK ALSO disrupts conventional thinking about immigration. For example, many people who want to reform immigration policy rely heavily on national legal systems to move forward. In the United States, this means seeing immigrants' rights as a matter of national belonging, and so as a matter of civil rights. This framework for assessing borders has produced meaningful change, but it can be incomplete or even counterproductive. In the United States, limiting the injustices done in the name of borders calls for blending approaches based on both national belonging and standards for treating any human being—sometimes going beyond what are often called human rights.

Other disruptive ideas target some distinctions that bring false clarity to immigration policy. It's tempting to distinguish sharply between refugees and economic migrants, between family or work migration, between temporary and permanent migration, and between lawful and unlawful presence. But responses to migration that rely on oversimplifying in these ways run a serious risk of limiting vision and enabling misguided policies.

Another area for fresh thinking: many people who support immigration don't take seriously enough the concern that newcomers will undermine or impair the lives of some of the destination country's citizens, including its historically disadvantaged groups. Long-time citizens may believe that newcomers take jobs and require services that cost more than the newcomers pay in taxes, or that some citizens lose out when newcomers arrive. Dismissing their voices out of hand—without testing their foundation and adopting remedies—can prompt skepticism or backlash, which in turn can mobilize cultural or racial prejudice.

I'll also try to disrupt the misleading intuition that questioning borders will lead to open borders, or to no borders at all. That's not true. Some parts of this book may suggest more migration across national borders in the short run, and possibly in the long run. But as I'll explain, the overall outcome will be levels of migration that are more sustainable and more broadly accepted.

A Few Disclaimers

Just as I've said something about my personal story, I should confess the professional perspectives that I bring to writing this book. I'm a lawyer by training, and I've been a law professor for over forty years. My experiences as a teacher, scholar, and occasional advocate have shaped my views. I believe that legal rules and institutions offer guidance on what justice requires. This grounding in law leads naturally to my focus on immigration policy and how to make it. But I know that this law-centered perspective can come with blinders.

First, justice goes well beyond formal obligations based on legal rules. Justice also demands cogent reasons for what's decided and what's done. Relatedly, focusing on the letter of the law can be confining and misleading. The law is often not what it seems to be. Law in action can differ a lot from law on the books. The law can become a cover for bad behavior by casting it as "legal" and so supposedly beyond question. When this happens, cruelty, discrimination, and subordination can become normal. But law can also be a lever for change and a force for good. Much of this book shows what's wrong with laws and policies, and why many of the best responses require efforts to change them.

Relatedly, law and legal institutions provide just one of many professional perspectives on migration. To be sure, law and legal institutions shape how immigration policy touches peoples' lives. And yet wisdom requires looking through the lenses of history, sociology, political science, economics, philosophy, religious studies, regional studies, literature, the arts, and more.

More fundamentally, professional perspectives on immigration run the risk of viewing human lives without listening to the voices of the people and communities directly affected. These voices aren't always in unison or harmony; they often conflict. But hearing them is essential. I've shared my personal story not just to help you interpret what I say in this book, but also because personal stories matter. Even if each is just one story of many millions, each story needs to be heard. Without listening to them, not much will change in attitudes, in culture, or in the lives of people and communities.

So this book is ambitious. I feel like a track and field athlete who chooses the decathlon, knowing that others are more practiced and accomplished in some other events than I am. And yet, I'm convinced that someone needs to combine different vantage points to lay the foundation for doing better.

WHO IS MY audience? My answer has three parts. First, I write for people who want to know more and are willing to think more. Some might share my perspectives on immigration policy, but they might still find it useful to ask what makes these perspectives persuasive or not. I also write for people who are uncertain about their views or who might approach my views with skepticism.

Second, I write for an audience broader than people who know about immigration policy. This book isn't just for specialists. I hope that all readers find it informative and thought-provoking. This book is for anyone who cares about human migration and wants to hear more about what might make immigration policy more consistent with fairness and justice.

Third, I write for readers worldwide. I rely heavily on examples from the United States. Maybe that's the way it should be. After all, that's what

I know best. But the questions at the heart of this book arise in some form virtually everywhere. The US experience offers lessons for many situations around the world where migration is or will be a fact of life. In short, I don't want what I write *about* to limit the audience that I write *for*.

A Roadmap

Here's a roadmap that lays out the ten questions that frame this book. Part I grounds the inquiry in a discussion of borders. Chapter 1 asks: Why national borders, and what might make them more fair and just? Chapter 2 probes how challenges to national borders can reflect the *humanity claims* that all people have. I'll focus on responses to forced migration. Chapter 3 discusses what I call the *belonging claims* of people who are part of communities in a country.

Part II applies the lessons of Part I to core questions of immigration policy. Chapter 4 asks: Who should be let in? Does it matter what countries they come from? Who should be kept out? Chapter 5 discusses whether newcomers stay temporarily or indefinitely. Who decides, and on what basis?

Part III explores how the law on the books is only part of what happens in reality. Chapter 6 inquires: Why do so many people lack lawful status? Should some people who are unlawfully in a country get lawful immigration status and a path to citizenship? Chapter 7 asks questions on the flipside. When is enforcement of immigration laws justified or unjust? Who should make enforcement decisions, and how?

Part IV delves into foundational issues. Chapter 8 asks: How might decision-makers respect anxieties that immigration can generate among other insiders? Chapter 9 probes what it means to address migration's root causes. What might give people a real choice to stay in their homes and in their countries—in other words, a choice *not* to move—but without just imposing more border control? Chapter 10 asks about the big picture for borders and belonging. What wrongs are done in the name of borders? How should immigration decisions be made? How does history matter? The Conclusion wraps up by returning to some foundational themes in the Introduction.

Two Approaches in Tension

I admit that this book reflects two approaches in tension with each other. One is realistic. The other is utopian. My goal is to blend them as much as possible, though that's not easy. This book may seem like it's written by two authors in honest conversation with each other. One accepts the constraints of coarse politics, and the other embraces noble ideas. That contrast and combination may not be a bad thing. This tension may be inherent in any effort to deal forthrightly with a complex topic that can prompt serious thought, controversy, and even polarization. Working with this tension between approaches, I try to sketch a realistic utopia to offer a framework for crucial choices.[1]

ON THE REALISTIC side of things: responses to migration must be sensitive to political context. War, famine, climate change, and many other factors will influence decisions by people to migrate or not. Government decisions must respond not only to these patterns of movement, but also to the political forces that migration can generate.

Some responses come from people who are anxious or deeply troubled when people don't comply with immigration laws. In today's world of nation-states, many people take national borders as a matter of faith without seriously questioning them. Other responses come from migrants and the people who welcome them. All of this shapes what is politically realistic.

The only quote that I've heard attributed to both Albert Einstein and Yogi Berra is this: "In theory, there is no difference between theory and practice, but in practice, there is." A realistic assessment of borders and immigration policy requires assuming a world of nation-states with borders of some sort. But working realistically, we can identify pragmatic steps—some small, yet positive—that can combine in the rough and tumble of nation-states and national politics. In each chapter, I'll identify ways to improve the conversation and concrete measures to move realistically toward a better version of what exists in the world.

WHAT ABOUT THE utopia in realistic utopia? I've mentioned fairness and justice. I realize that not everyone will share my perspective on these terms as they apply to migration, but here it is. As Chapter 1 will explain, my utopia can have national borders, but only if they respect these two ideas. Some readers might use *ethical* as an overall label for the borders that I favor. This label can be useful, but it's distracting to get into academic debates about different approaches to ethics. Instead, I'll rely on two core ideas.

The first idea is respect for what I'm calling *humanity claims*. These claims are based on the dignity of all people, no matter who they are or where they live. Humanity claims reflect the idea that borders must not be used to inflict injuries that no human being should suffer. I realize that the notion of *realistic* utopia does a lot of work here. Some people might believe that no human being should ever suffer *any* consequences of national borders, including restrictions on freedom of movement. But I'm asking a narrower question: Given that national borders restrict some movement, when do restrictions in the name of national borders go too far?

Humanity claims set a floor or minimum as a way of thinking about justice for all people, regardless of their ties to any countries. This respect for dignity can find expression in the language of human rights. But human rights can refer to something narrower than what I mean. Human rights can imply rights recognized by international or national law, or by legislatures, courts, or other institutions. Human rights can refer to a certain type of academic analysis, or to the obligations that governments owe to people under their authority. Instead, I use the term humanity claims as a way of writing more broadly about the claims that all people have—simply because they are human beings—to challenge harm that they suffer.

The second core idea is respect for what I'll call *belonging claims*. These are claims grounded in the connections that people have to communities in any given country. These ties are the source of their claims—often even if they don't have lawful immigration status—to be treated like others with connections to communities in the country. This might not mean treatment that's fully or immediately equal. But national borders must take these belonging claims seriously.

Belonging claims and humanity claims are conceptually distinct. In some settings, both can be persuasive. For example, objecting to harsh conditions of immigration detention—while government authorities decide about deporting someone—can be both a humanity claim and a belonging claim if the person being detained is a long-time resident of that country. Harsh conditions may be an unacceptable way to treat any person, and especially unacceptable for long-time residents.

BELONGING CLAIMS AND humanity claims combine to make sure that national borders and immigration policy reflect the voices of people who have often been ignored or silenced. Those voices deserve to be heard, even assuming that the world consists of nation-states. This doesn't mean that these voices always win out. Some outcomes will stay the same, and others will change. What matters is who is taken into account in making decisions about migration.

Do borders that meet this standard exist in the world today? I don't know of any national borders without flaws. But some are better or worse than others. From this book's overall perspective, this depends on how national borders respect—or don't respect—humanity claims and belonging claims as the result of decisions that people with power make every single day.

My sketch of realistic utopia suggests steps that are incremental, but these steps reflect hope and vision rather than despair or resignation. Sometimes the only way to move policy toward the utopian is first to work for what's realistic. The specifics of progress will change from setting to setting, and over time. What matters is that each step reflects a long-term vision of something better than what prevails today. This matters not just for immigration policy, but also for making sure that gridlock in immigration policy doesn't fetter other areas of public policy—such as the economy, education, social welfare, the environment, or international relations, to name just a few areas of concern and debate.

If I dare to consider what a world would look like if it embraced my thinking in this book, national borders would no longer enable or mask oppression. But national borders would still exist for the good that they can do—to shape identities and cultures, and to give people a sense of control and agency over their lives. The result would not be doing away with national borders, but instead making them much more open for more people than those borders are today. This book is a guide toward that world—the world that I want my grandchildren to inherit.

PART I

Borders and Claims

I

Why National Borders,
and Why Not?

When talking about immigration, a few basic questions might arise. Why national borders? Should national borders exist? Why or why not? Why not open borders? These are important questions, though they might surprise some people who assume that national borders are so well-established today that questioning them is pointless. I'll start by explaining that national borders are just one type of boundary. This fact opens up thinking about justifications for national borders—not just to be realistic, but because borders can work for good.

For all of human history, borders of many types have created insiders and outsiders. But national borders in their current form are modern inventions. Earlier line-drawing was typically based on something else. Lines may have marked allegiance to a feudal lord or membership in a religious community or a tribe. But over the past half-millennium, borders have come to mark off one nation-state from another. National governments as ruling sovereigns came to demand allegiance and define membership. They use borders to let some people in, to keep out others, and sometimes to keep people in.

Many skeptics of national borders see them as hoarding prosperity for a few and denying a fair share to people on the wrong side of the line. Other skeptics ask: Why should someone's birthplace matter so much?[1] Why does so much depend on your parents' nationality? A related perspective notes the origins of national borders in conquest and colonization at the hands of empires and settlers. To consider national borders in light of these questions and these skepticisms, let's think more about boundaries in general.

Boundaries in Other Settings

National borders create bounded communities. As boundaries, they have much in common with other boundaries in daily life. None of my examples are quite like national borders. Some are private boundaries, not public ones. People with guns may enforce national borders, but not some of my examples of boundaries. The reasons for other boundaries may not apply to national borders. But my point here is more basic: that boundaries of many types are part of life in complex societies, and that boundaries reflect contested values and choices.

Consider admissions policies for colleges and universities. Some are open to all applicants with a high school diploma or GED certificate. But most admit some students and exclude others. The goal is a better student experience on the inside. Selectivity might strive for the best combination of students to enrich discussions, or try to admit only students who are adequately prepared, given limited space and other resources.

These policies can be controversial, perhaps because selection criteria may be misguided. Debated are standardized tests, affirmative action, and the mix of residents and nonresidents at public institutions. But critiques target *how* to select, not *whether* to select. Some may argue that these admissions policies aren't like national borders because colleges and universities admit based on merit. But the ways to decide merit have been controversial, so what remains is a boundary and how to draw it.

The boundary around a family's home is another example. Whether it's a house, an apartment, or a car, few would doubt that a family can set up a perimeter that includes some people as part of the family, admits others as guests, and keeps out strangers. The boundary of a home prompts questions. When and how can someone repel intruders? When and how may the government surveil the home? Who is an insider protected by the home's boundary? Does the perimeter conceal abuse within? But these questions about *how* to draw a home's boundary assume that some sort of boundary is justified for reasons that include providing a space for relationships based on nurturing and security.

Some may say that families differ from national borders because exclusion from a family requires no justification. You don't have to let me into your family, and if you keep me out, you don't need to explain why. But this doesn't persuasively distinguish the family. Some people believe that a country is also a closed community that can exclude without explanation. Many decisions of the US Supreme Court reflect this approach to exclusion. To some observers, families and countries might not be so different.

A different sort of example: state lines in the United States that mark off the territory of one state from the next. Unlike boundaries around educational institutions and families, the boundaries between states are open to US citizens who want to cross them. But importantly, they are still boundaries that define a type of belonging. This can matter, for example, when states act to adopt policies at odds with the federal government—as when they adopt what are sometimes called sanctuary policies. Boundaries between states can also provide some sense of identity, culture, agency, and pride.

One last but very meaningful example is membership in indigenous tribes within nation-states. Here, too, the rules that define membership combine to allow the formation of identity, culture, agency, and pride. They nurture members and allow them to have a voice. All of this would be far weaker without the boundary of the tribe. Much of the violence and oppression that Native Nations have suffered in the course of history reflects the abject failure to respect Native boundaries.

Moving Toward Better Borders

Throughout history, affinity groups have conferred benefits on their members. But affinity groups have also marginalized other people, often based on race, religion, gender, or class. These were often the basis of subordination before national borders became the predominant framework for power and politics,. The end of national borders can let old hostilities and hatreds emerge, as in former Yugoslavia in the 1990s.

Why would national borders do better? It depends on whether national borders can provide the concepts, the vocabulary, the laws, and the institutions to minimize, dismantle, or prevent subordination. The problem, it goes without saying, is that the project of building fair societies within national borders is far from complete. Although constitutions and similar documents in many countries reflect some intent to limit injustice, they fail in many ways.

National borders are the Achilles heel of a fair and just society. National borders aren't the only problem, but they are nefarious because they often cause damage that's subtle or invisible. The reason is the belief that different rules can apply when governments implement national borders. Think about checking documents, conducting searches, arresting people, and applying deadly force. National borders often mark off lawless zones, or zones of exception, where decisions and decisionmakers can avoid the scrutiny or constraints that apply when national borders aren't involved.[2] National borders can make cruelty and discrimination seem normal.

As I explained in the Introduction, national borders can escape this dilemma only by respecting both humanity claims and belonging claims. Humanity claims are based on what all people should expect. Belonging claims are based on belonging to communities in the country. These two types of claims are distinct from each other, though they can overlap and are sometimes confused with each other. Each type isn't enough by itself, but together they can show the way to better borders.

Humanity Claims

The core idea behind humanity claims is that all people deserve respect and protection. Humanity claims don't depend on ties with any particular country that someone might or might not have. Instead, the idea is that *all* human beings have dignity that deserves respect. This idea often appears in discussions of human rights, which offer one way of articulating humanity claims. For example, the 1948 Universal Declaration of Human Rights opens by citing the "equal and inalienable rights of all members of the human family" and affirms the "inherent dignity" of people.[3] Some ways of enforcing national borders violate human dignity. This means that they disrespect humanity claims. I'll provide examples in later chapters, but here are a few from some aspects of immigration enforcement by the US government.

It's an affront to human dignity to separate children from parents as a way to deter and punish border crossings. Disrespect for dignity is also the problem with border walls that shunt migrants into burning deserts where they face a serious risk of death from heat, thirst, cold, or starvation, or of serious injuries from long falls. Prolonged detention in immigration prisons—often for an indefinite period of time—is also an affront to human dignity.[4]

Not all will agree that all of these examples reflect disrespect for humanity claims. Some might argue that severe restrictions on migration are justified because people who choose to migrate outside lawful channels bring enforcement-related hardships upon themselves. Other people might take the opposite view: that any restriction on movement gives rise to a persuasive humanity claim challenging that restriction.

People will debate where to draw the line between persuasive and unpersuasive humanity claims against different aspects of immigration policy. But my point for now is more foundational than where exactly to draw that line. Instead, I'm suggesting that this is a way of understanding protections for all people—as basic to humanity and not depending on whether the affected people have attachments to the country that is implementing its national borders.

Belonging Claims

In contrast to the humanity claims of all people, other claims are grounded in belonging to communities in the country. These belonging claims follow naturally from the view that borders foster good things on the inside. If that's true, then people who are part of communities in the country should get their share of those good things. Their claims come not from being human beings, but from being insiders. In other words, insiders have some persuasive claims that outsiders generally can't make.[5]

One basic belonging claim is that insiders deserve the same respect as other insiders. This doesn't mean that all insiders must be treated identically. Some differences in treatment may be justified, especially if differences fade over time. But it's wrong to dismiss their claims out of hand without close scrutiny. Any possible justifications for differences require close examination. It's essential to make sure that a difference isn't just a cover for impermissible discrimination against some insiders.

For example: imagine a law that makes it easier for citizens of Norwegian ancestry—as compared to citizens of Nigerian ancestry—to sponsor close relatives to immigrate to join them. Or suppose it's harder for Muslim citizens—than for citizens who are Christians, Jews, or atheists—to sponsor a noncitizen spouse. Such unequal treatment based on nationality, ethnicity, race, or religion might unjustifiably prefer some insiders over others. Insiders with no connections to the disfavored countries would get better treatment than other insiders. The disfavored insiders might have spouses from Nigeria or from targeted majority-Muslim countries. Or the disfavored insiders may be US companies hoping to hire employees or US universities hoping to admit students from those countries.

As these cases show, it's simple-minded to think that national borders only protect insider-citizens from outsider-newcomers. This view of immigration restrictions is widely held, but it's wrong. Though some insiders are skeptical or hostile toward newcomers, other insiders welcome their arrival. Immigration policy should reflect what emerges from these views. Insiders who favor new arrivals may not always prevail, but it's essential to consider the interests of all insiders. The complexity of any decision to prefer some insiders over others makes it all the more important to undertake it with care after considering the views of *all* insiders.

Integration and Belonging

Essential to all insiders getting the same respect is having the belonging of all insiders fostered, not marginalized. This means that as newcomers become part of communities in the country, it's vital to integrate them over time.[6] Integration is the essential foundation for respecting belonging claims. Relatedly, the purpose and the measure of successful integration is strong civic solidarity in the country as a whole.[7]

Given this purpose, integration must be a mutually respectful and inclusive process that doesn't prefer the belonging claims of some insiders over the belonging claims of other insiders. This means avoiding the sort of coerced assimilation that forces some newcomers—but not others—to submerge their cultures and languages. If that begrudging approach to integration prevails, the integration of newcomers over time will vary by their country of origin, with advantages for some insiders but not for others.

This perspective on integration explains why discriminatory obstacles to integration are so troubling. In the first half of the twentieth century, some state laws in the United States barred some noncitizens from owning land if they were "ineligible to citizenship." These laws didn't expressly discriminate by race, but they targeted noncitizens of Asian ancestry.[8] Only in 1952 did US law no longer have any racial restrictions on US citizenship through naturalization.

These land laws undermined integration long after these newcomers—and their US-born citizen children—had become part of communities in the United States. This type of law has reappeared a century later. In 2023, Florida adopted a law forbidding some noncitizens from owning much of the land in the state, with extra penalties on violators from China.[9]

INTEGRATION AS RESPECT for belonging claims requires not just recognition of integration after it occurs, but also a public commitment to foster integration. What is the difference? In the United States and many other countries, legal status often recognizes a newcomer's integration only after it has occurred. Naturalization requires showing the acquisition of some knowledge of English and of history and civics. Only then does naturalization recognize that integration.

Better are laws and policies that foster integration actively, not just recognize it. An example is the US Constitution's Fourteenth Amendment, which confers citizenship on almost all children born on US soil. Citizenship for these children can't guarantee their integration, but it can make a big difference by fostering integration, especially if their parents have no lawful status.[10] Another example is making naturalization easier. Immigrants who become citizens are more likely to integrate, especially if they don't fit the stereotypes associated with the dominant culture. Similarly, dual citizenship can foster integration by making it easier for newcomers to leave old ties behind and forge new ones where they live. Dual citizenship for parents can also ease integration for their children. Having parents with citizenship is likely to fortify children's sense of belonging in the country where they grow up.[11]

IF WE CONSIDER humanity claims and belonging claims as approaches to assessing borders, we can look more concretely at ways these approaches have applied in specific settings. In the next chapter, I'll look at migrants who decide that they need to escape dire conditions and at the humanity claims that these forced migrants may have.

2

What Are Better Responses to Forced Migration?

In the 2010s and 2020s, large numbers of migrants have crossed national borders—or they have tried. They have fled civil war, famine, climate change, natural disasters, collapsing economies, oppressive governments, and other dire conditions. In the United States, many of these migrants come from Central America, Haiti, and Venezuela, but many others come long distances from all over the world. In Europe, many migrants have left behind political and economic instability and armed conflict in the Middle East, in Africa, or in Afghanistan. In Asia, the Rohingya fleeing Myanmar are just one of many large and small migrations across national borders. Similar scenes are familiar worldwide. Climate change–related flooding, drought, and famine as drivers of migration seem especially likely to grow in impact.[1]

How should a destination country treat people when circumstances displace them and they feel forced to leave their own country? For any given situation, it's reasonable to debate whether the circumstances are severe enough, and whether migrants are truly forced to cross a national border. But many people accept—at least in principle—that destination countries should protect some people in these situations.[2]

I'm calling people "forced migrants" if they have left their countries because dire conditions or some threat of harm displaced them, or if they would face those conditions or harm if they had to go back. Often they seek protection in a country where they have few immediate ties, so they aren't insiders because they aren't part of any communities in that country. This means that many forced migrants can't make persuasive belonging claims to challenge the enforcement of national borders against them. But forced migrants can have humanity claims for protection in spite of laws and policies that try to limit their mobility. To explore the treatment of forced migrants from this perspective, I'll start with the evolution of protection for refugees since World War II.

Refugee Protection Since World War II

Today, migrants who win recognition as "refugees" gain favorable treatment under an international protection system that arose after World War II. Before the war, many countries had turned away people who later perished in the Holocaust. The aftermath of the war saw the displacement of millions of people. The collective response of many countries led to the protection system now widespread in much of the Global North.[3]

This system's centerpiece is an international treaty: the 1951 Geneva Convention Relating to the Status of Refugees.[4] Its terms reflect its origins in the chaos and suffering of postwar Europe. In fact, the Convention originally limited its scope to migrants displaced by "events occurring in Europe before 1 January 1951." Even though a cataclysmic conflict had ended, new geopolitical chasms had opened and threatened to persist. What's now a textured body of human rights law had not yet emerged.[5] In this setting, the Convention established an approach that came to shape debate over the reception of forced migrants in much of the world. This is true even though most of the countries that take in the vast majority of forced migrants today are not Convention signatories.

The Convention's basic protection is nonreturn or *nonrefoulement*. Countries must not return anyone to any other country where they would face persecution on account of nationality, race, religion, political opinion, or membership in a particular social group. This is the Convention definition of refugee. The Convention put into a formal agreement the general principle that national borders must respect the humanity claims of forced migrants seeking protection. This principle doesn't mean that all forced migrants get asylum, but it's the conceptual framework for deciding if they do.

Countries that are parties to the Convention typically have incorporated its basic protections into their own national laws. This means that people who seek recognition as refugees invoke not just the Convention, but also the laws of the country where they seek protection. These national laws often offer more than bare nonreturn. In the United States, for example, government officials may exercise discretion to grant asylum to anyone who reaches or crosses the US border and qualifies as a refugee. With an asylum grant, migrants and their spouses and children may work. After one year they can become lawful permanent residents, and later they can become citizens.[6]

The Convention's definition of refugee is narrow, protecting only some forced migrants. To qualify as a refugee—and thus get asylum in many countries—requires navigating a complex process. For example, the US asylum statute adopts the Convention's wording by requiring applicants to show a type and degree of harm that counts as "persecution." Harm must be "on account of" nationality, race, religion, political opinion, or membership in a particular social group. Each of these five grounds has a complex definition. Some people who seem to qualify are still ineligible for some or all of the protection that might be available—for example, if they missed a deadline to apply, if they have a criminal conviction, or if they have been persecutors themselves.[7]

To understand the complexity of this definition of refugee, it's helpful to know that the Convention's drafters viewed its basic duty of nonreturn as an exception, not a challenge, to independent countries' sovereign control of their national borders. The definition of refugee has limited the number of people that the Convention protects. Countries can be more generous if they want to be. As the Cold War took hold, this system left the United States and Western European countries the latitude to recognize people as refugees from Communism if they managed to leave the Soviet Union or its satellites. In contrast, the Convention left countries free not to protect the many people who don't qualify as refugees. But many are still forced migrants—people who felt they had no choice but to leave their original countries to escape war, famine, civil disorder, environmental disaster, or other calamities.[8]

Some applicants denied asylum because they are not refugees may get other protections. One is basic nonreturn without asylum. In the United States, this is called withholding of removal. In addition, the Convention Against Torture (CAT) bars return to any country where a migrant faces treatment that amounts to torture by the government. Withholding and CAT protection don't provide the durable status and benefits of asylum. They don't cover spouses and children. They don't routinely lead to permanent residence or citizenship. Migrants might later lose withholding or CAT protection if conditions change in the country where they originally faced harm.[9]

CAN PEOPLE STILL apply for a country's protection if they don't reach that country's border? Yes; many countries that are parties to the Convention—and many countries that aren't—also give some refugees who are far outside the country official permission to enter. In the United States, refugees admitted from outside the country routinely become permanent residents, and many become citizens. Unlike refugees who get asylum, they get modest amounts of government financial support.[10]

In the United States, the president consults with Congress each year to set a limit on refugee admissions, split among regions of the world. In the early twenty-first century, the annual limit fluctuated between 70,000 and 100,000. The Trump administration slashed it each year, down to 18,000 for 2020. The Biden administration reversed the trend by setting annual limits of 125,000 starting in 2021, still a tiny fraction of the worldwide need. The deliberate crippling of administrative capacity during the Trump years left actual admissions slow to recover.[11]

Practical control of numbers is the biggest political difference between refugees admitted from outside the country and refugees granted asylum at the border or inside the country. For refugee admissions, governments can adopt strict selection criteria and set numerical limits, taking only a few of the tens of millions of people worldwide who might qualify.

Choosing refugees from outside the country is extremely selective and discretionary, based on regional political context, degree of threat, and ties to the country offering protection. Disappointed applicants are far away and can do almost nothing to reverse rejections. Asylum is different. Countries of potential asylum don't limit the number of approvals. When many asylum seekers reach a country's borders, governments face serious challenges—humanitarian, practical, and political.

Protection Under Stress

The favorable treatment of people who qualify as refugees contrasts with meager protection for the tens of millions of forced migrants who fall outside the refugee definition. A big part of public opinion in many potential asylum countries reflects some impulse to protect forced migrants, but the domestic political viability of protection is delicate.

For asylum to be politically viable, one precondition is public confidence that the system can decide who is a refugee. Because it's so hard to apply the Convention definition of refugee and identify who qualifies for protection, the protection system is fragile.[12] A related precondition for domestic political viability involves numbers. If too many people seek asylum as refugees, it may seem like an admissions boulevard. As a matter of politics, asylum must coexist with other ways to let in newcomers. This view of refugees and asylum requires that protection be characterized as an exceptional act of sovereign grace. According to this view, recognition as a refugee must not be seen as a matter of right that could undermine control over national borders.[13]

Until recently, barriers to long-distance travel kept millions of forced migrants away from Europe, the United States, and other potential asylum countries. For over fifty years after World War II, exit controls in the Soviet Union and Eastern Europe made it impossible for many from those countries to seek asylum in the West. Today, many forced migrants bound for distant countries must make harrowing journeys across jungles, deserts, and treacherous seas.[14]

These facts have tempted governments in the Global North to assume that few forced migrants would reach their physical borders, and that most forced migrants would stay indefinitely in countries closer to their original homes. Indeed, most forced migrants go no further than neighboring countries. As of 2022, low and middle-income countries hosted 76 percent of refugees and other people in need of international protection. Over half of the world's forced migrants are in just seven countries. This imbalance largely reflects conscious efforts by countries in the Global North to keep forced migrants from their borders.[15]

But geographic insulation is unreliable. Many forced migrants are reaching Global North countries where some people view them with suspicion or hostility. On the US–Mexico border, people from El Salvador, Guatemala, and Honduras come in growing numbers. So do people from countries around the world, ranging from Senegal to China to Ukraine. Countries of potential asylum in Europe have seen a broad array of countries of origin.[16]

Public figures and media can treat the number of arrivals as a matter of border control, not as challenges of humanitarian reception and of addressing the causes of forced migration. In turn, perceptions of threats to border security have become central to politics in many potential asylum countries. Notions of border crisis can amplify narratives of asylum claims as fabricated, and of asylum seekers as criminals. Some observers in a potential asylum country may view protection of forced migrants—even if they qualify as refugees—as altruism that the country can't afford.

Managing and Limiting Protection

In this political climate, governments have taken steps to manage protection, typically with the effect of limiting it. The United States and other countries have blocked access to protection while maintaining a veneer of compliance with the Refugee Convention. These responses have made the most of the Convention's near-silence on how to implement protection, thus keeping forced migrants in the Global South.[17]

One technique is interdiction—stopping migrants in international waters before they can reach a potential asylum country. The US Coast Guard has long kept forced migrants from Haiti, Cuba, and elsewhere away from US shores. In the Mediterranean, the governments of potential asylum countries keep boats with forced migrants away from continental Europe and sometimes imprison those who still get there. Australia combines interdiction with long-term imprisonment of asylum seekers in Papua New Guinea and Nauru. Closely related is the practice of channeling migrants to perilous routes with risk to life and limb.[18]

Relatedly, some countries effectively push their national borders outward by requiring asylum seekers to apply in the first "safe country" that they reach. In the United States, the Trump administration issued a regulation that barred asylum applications from anyone who traveled through another country without applying for asylum there.[19] This sort of asylum rule is an example of allowing countries to push their borders out to the borders of neighboring countries.

The same idea drives a more aggressive version of this approach that enlists other countries to restrict the transit of asylum seekers. For example, the European Union has an agreement with Turkey to keep migrants from reaching Greece and other EU countries. Several countries in the EU have arranged with Libya, Morocco, Tunisia, Niger, and other countries in Africa to limit northward migration. The EU has an agreement with Lebanon to prevent boat travel from Lebanon to Cyprus, where forced migrants would find it easier to reach the EU. The United States enlists Mexico to keep migrants from travelling northward through Mexico to the United States.[20] These arrangements typically call for substantial payments or other forms of compensation to the other countries that are partners in this strategy.[21]

Restrictions like interdiction, safe third-country rules, and agreements with transit countries rely on a vast network for regulating transnational travel. Visa requirements impede direct travel by the vast majority of forced migrants from their countries of origin to potential asylum countries. Private companies help enforce these requirements. Governments impose penalties on carriers that don't check documents before letting migrants onto planes, busses, ships, or other conveyances.[22]

IF FORCED MIGRANTS reach destination countries, other restrictive measures may kick in. They start with border enforcement methods, some of which are callous, cruel, or administered in a discriminatory way. Examples include separating children from parents, detaining migrants under severe conditions, and criminal charges for unlawful entry.[23]

Beyond enforcement itself, governments have curtailed the processes for deciding asylum applications. Since the late 1990s, most asylum seekers at US borders or ports of entry get only a shortened process called "expedited removal." They don't get a full asylum hearing unless they convince a government official in an interview that they have a "credible fear" of persecution. Many asylum seekers must navigate this process soon after being put in a detention facility, and few have the help of a lawyer.[24]

More recently, the Trump administration arranged with several countries in Central America to let the US government shunt asylum seekers there. Other measures restrict access to asylum for anyone who reaches a country's border. In 2018, the Trump administration adopted a policy—officially the Migrant Protection Protocols—that required many asylum seekers to remain in Mexico for long periods, often under unsafe conditions, before they could pursue their asylum applications in the United States. In 2020, the Trump administration used the COVID-19 pandemic and a public health statute, Title 42, to close the US–Mexico border to many asylum seekers.[25]

President Biden took office in 2021 after making campaign promises to reverse Trump policies on immigration, including asylum. His administration's efforts to rescind the Migrant Protection Protocols and the Title 42 border closure met with resistance from the federal courts, but the Migrant Protection Protocols ended in 2022 after the Mexican government announced that it would no longer accept people processed under the program. The Title 42 closure ended in 2023, when the Biden administration declared the end of the public health emergency.[26]

Some Biden administration policies toward forced migrants have much in common with Trump policies. According to a 2023 Biden regulation, asylum seekers must apply at ports of entry after using a mobile phone app to make an appointment at one of a relatively small number of available times. The regulation presumes that anyone who doesn't follow this procedure after traveling through another country— in practical terms, Mexico—without applying for asylum there is ineligible for asylum. The Biden administration imposed a more severe border closure in June 2024, limiting asylum applications to exceptional cases.[27]

OTHER EFFORTS TO limit asylum have narrowed the legal definition of refugee, especially by tightening what counts as persecution on account of membership in a particular social group. In the Trump administration, Attorney General Jeff Sessions issued rulings that restricted asylum based on domestic violence or gang violence and expanded the use of discretionary denials of asylum. Under Biden, Attorney General Merrick Garland vacated these rulings. But tightening requirements and allowing more discretionary denials—along with other techniques like expanding bars to asylum and demanding more proof—remain tools for asylum skeptics.[28]

These methods for managing (and limiting) protection have one thing in common. All are ways for potential asylum countries to treat asylum as a matter of sovereign grace. The reasons for managing protection include the view that it is a scarce resource that shouldn't be used too readily. Managing protection can also reflect deep skepticism of asylum or the view, as Donald Trump put it, that asylum is a scam that must yield to a "nation first" policy to ward off foreign threats.[29] But national borders enable injustice if they shut out people who urgently need protection. People who may have persuasive humanity claims must have a way to make those claims. This means that it's essential to have an honest conversation about possible approaches to protection.

Approaches to Protection

The first step in this conversation is to ask: How has the protection system reflected in the Refugee Convention become so inadequate and so inaccessible as a way of respecting humanity claims of migrants? The answer lies in the system's bedrock assumption: a line between two groups of migrants—refugees who qualify for protection and other migrants who don't. This assumption reflects a condition for the system's political acceptability. Protection must stay narrow as an exception to national borders. This has meant defining refugee narrowly and limiting access to asylum.

Reality is messier. The line between refugees and other migrants is very hard to draw. People migrate for many combinations of reasons. Some cases may seem clear, such as a political activist who voices a public position that their home country government moves to punish. These activists fit the archetype of a refugee that the Convention should protect. Also clear is that other people have no plausible claim to protection under the Convention. They can stay where they are without hardship but want to cross national borders, perhaps to find better employment.[30]

But many cases are in the gray area in between. These are the cases that put great stress on the process of granting or denying protection. Cases are complex enough to defy simple sorting. Many people who might qualify as refugees don't get a fair chance to apply. They may not have the lawyer's help that they need to present their cases. Applicants may lack essential financial resources or adequate time to gather evidence. They are often held in detention, which limits their ability to apply effectively. It's essential to dismantle these barriers. These gray area cases are also numerous enough to require better resourced systems to decide fairly.

MORE FUNDAMENTALLY, BETTER process will only go so far as a solution. What about a broader refugee definition? Two regional agreements offer models. The Organization of African Unity's Refugee Convention of 1969 moved away from risk of persecution as the touchstone. It said that someone can be a refugee based on a broader list of factors that include "external aggression, occupation, foreign domination or events seriously disturbing public order in either part or the whole of his country of origin or nationality."[31]

In South America, the Cartagena Declaration on Refugees of 1984 also defines refugee more broadly. It provides that refugees are people who have "fled their country because their lives, security or freedom have been threatened by generalized violence, foreign aggression, internal conflicts, massive violation of human rights or other circumstances which have seriously disturbed public order."[32]

These two refugee definitions have been the basis for protecting large groups of forced migrants on some basis—though without formal recognition of refugee status and a grant of asylum with durable residence. In practical terms, even if it's a political nonstarter to change the refugee definition in the Convention itself, these broader definitions may show the way toward protecting forced migrants without recognizing them as refugees.

PROTECTION FOR FORCED migrants also requires fundamental rethinking. Here I'll focus on what individual countries can and should do, and I'll turn later in this book to transnational cooperation. Rethinking should start by recognizing that the Geneva Convention definition of refugee, even if expanded, is ill-suited to forced migration that's both large-scale and worldwide. The problem isn't that the Geneva Convention arose in a Eurocentric framing in the first phase of the Cold War. The real challenge is how to deal with forced migration that's the tragic consequence of wars, civil disorder, religious and ethnic strife, natural disasters, climate change, and more.[33] Many forced migrants won't fit an expanded definition of refugee, but they are still in dire straits. Not all humanity claims will be persuasive, but they deserve to be taken seriously.

Beyond the definition of refugee, it's vital to consider what protection could mean in alternative forms, and what the process should be for deciding about protection. I'll begin with alternative forms of protection that don't offer the immediate durable resettlement that asylum confers, but which may be available differently—to more people or more quickly, or both.

Protection in the European Union is instructive. A Qualification Directive, first issued in 2004 and amended in 2011, set out rules governing how EU countries should interpret and apply the Refugee Convention. For people who don't qualify as refugees, the Directive created "subsidiary protection"—also called "complementary protection." It protects against return to a country where migrants would face the death penalty or execution, or torture or inhumane or degrading treatment or punishment.

Importantly for rethinking protection, the Directive also prohibits return to a country where migrants would face "serious and individual threat to a civilian's life or person by reason of indiscriminate violence in situations of international or internal armed conflict."[34] This coverage reflects an attempt to respect the humanity claims of forced migrants based on their need for protection. Initial grants are one year, renewable in two-year increments. The broad coverage resembles the African Convention and the Cartagena Declaration, but in contrast the Qualification Directive has an established enforcement regime.[35]

In the United States, Temporary Protected Status (TPS) protects forced migrants (and the undocumented) against return even if they wouldn't qualify as refugees. TPS lets noncitizens stay and work, initially for renewable eighteen-month periods, if their countries are beset with armed conflict, environmental disaster, or other extraordinary and temporary conditions. The TPS statute became law in 1990, but the US government has used similar programs—Extended Voluntary Departure and Deferred Enforced Departure—since 1960.[36] As of 2024, TPS designations were active for sixteen countries, most recently Venezuela, Myanmar, Ukraine, Afghanistan, Cameroon, and Ethiopia. TPS is usually only for people already in the United States when their countries were designated, though people who came after the initial designation can be included if that designation is renewed.[37]

TPS doesn't lead directly to lawful permanent resident status or a path to citizenship. But some people have had TPS for many years or even several decades. TPS holders can become lawful permanent residents in other ways that emerge while they have TPS—perhaps through asylum or qualifying in an admission category based on family or work. Some become lawful permanent residents as the parents of their US-born citizen children, once those children turn twenty-one.[38]

WHERE CAN FORCED migrants seek protection? Must they first reach the countries where they seek protection? The answer is yes for subsidiary protection in the EU and TPS in the United States—and for asylum, too. This means that the people most able to access these forms of protection are those who have the strength, the means, and the luck for the journey. They aren't necessarily the people who are most in need. This means that these forms of protection might respect the humanity claims of some but disregard the humanity claims of many others.

An alternative is the approach in the EU's Temporary Protection Directive, which allows forced migrants to enter from outside the EU. It identifies five categories of people for temporary protection: Convention refugees, people who have fled armed conflict or endemic violence, people at serious risk of systemic and generalized human rights violations, and "others entitled to international protection." The EU adopted this Directive in 2001 but activated it for the first time in early 2022 for the several million people who fled Ukraine after Russia invaded. The Directive allows travel to any EU country, not just to the first EU country that people reach. The country where they seek protection must provide access to education, medical care, and other social services.[39]

The US government used a similar alternative for Afghans in 2021 and for Ukrainians in 2022, allowing them to apply outside the United States for permission to enter. This approach later expanded in October 2022 to include Venezuela, then in January 2023 to include Cuba, Haiti, and Nicaragua—for a total of 30,000 per month. These migrants enter with a status known as parole. It doesn't offer the path to lawful permanent residence and citizenship that comes with refugee admissions and asylum. And the program for Cuba, Haiti, Nicaragua, and Venezuela—known as the CHNV program—requires a financial sponsor in the United States, a passport, and the money to get to the United States after approval. But in broader terms, parole resembles other alternatives to asylum in giving forced migrants limited permission to stay.[40]

THESE ALTERNATIVES TO asylum deserve sober assessment. On the one hand, in different ways they allow a broader group of forced migrants to present their humanity claims, even if not all will be successful. And they allow forced migrants to seek protection without having to reach the country where they seek protection. This takes fiscal and political pressure off the physical border. Forced migrants can spread out to many locations, where relatives, churches, nonprofit organizations, or lawyers are more likely to give them support that they need to get on their feet. Work permits are typically available, depending on the program, and access to the job market is more likely where they have a support network.

The basic shortcoming of alternatives to asylum is that they are only temporary and don't provide stable long-term residence, at least not at first. In some parts of the world, many forced migrants have lived in "temporary" camps for more than a generation. Denying displaced people and their children any stable residence can deny them the opportunity to live full lives. In this way, temporary or precarious protection may disrespect the humanity claims of forced migrants.[41]

Other concerns are not with the alternatives themselves, but with how they fit into overall responses to forced migration. One concern is that governments offer alternatives only selectively to groups that are favored for reasons that reflect geopolitics or racial discrimination, but which don't address the needs of forced migrants even-handedly. Another concern is the use of alternatives to asylum to justify restrictions on asylum itself. When the Biden administration expanded parole from outside its border, it also limited access to asylum at the border. But many forced migrants have access to neither asylum nor any alternatives.

Finding Better Responses

In short, the current worldwide system exaggerates the clarity of the refugee-migrant line. It uses alternatives to asylum only selectively, and it underappreciates problems with those alternatives. But could a more fundamental reassessment beyond these alternatives lead to more respect for humanity claims in ways that might be politically realistic? I think so.

One fundamental choice is between making protection decisions for individuals or instead for groups. Some forced migrants have persuasive humanity claims to protection. Even if not all forced migrants do, an essential aspect of respecting humanity claims is getting a fair decision about that claim. Generally, the current asylum system calls on government officials to decide if a person or a family fits the refugee definition. The outcome depends on factors that vary widely but often have little to do with the strength of the claim. Which official will assess evidence and apply the refugee definition? Can asylum seekers get competent assistance? Will they be detained under conditions that make it hard to apply?

A partial solution might be giving individuals broader access to lawyers, but protection on a nationality or group basis may be a fuller response that's more attainable politically, more cost-effective, and more true to the facts. Local conditions can displace people from their home countries without meaningful variations among the displaced. Attention to the facts of specific cases applies a veneer of rationality, masking peripheral factors that cause outcomes to vary—such as who decides, the skill of lawyers, perceptions about credibility, and implicit bias. This advantage of a shift to group determinations is a lesson from TPS and parole programs forced migrants.[42]

ANOTHER FOCUS SHOULD be the line between refugees and migrants. Part of the problem, as I explained earlier in this chapter, is that the line is often too hard to apply with the confidence that would be appropriate, given the momentous consequences of falling on one side or the other. A deeper problem is that protecting forced migrants and responding to all migration are closely related, and even overlap. Refugees and other migrants are people who move, even as protection systems try to sort them apart. This means it's essential to harmonize responses to forced migrants with other migration pathways, such as for workers, that aren't usually seen as ways to protect forced migrants.[43]

Immigration policy that considers all migrants would reflect a truth that's too often overlooked. Forced migrants aren't just survivors in flight. They are multidimensional people who will shape the societies where they, their children, and their grandchildren settle. Forced migrants who don't qualify as refugees may be strong candidates for admission through other pathways based on family or work.[44]

The overlap between protecting forced migrants and attracting migrants to work has a long history. Soon after World War II, the United Kingdom recruited as workers over 90,000 displaced people from the Baltics, the Balkans, and central and eastern Europe. Decades later in Germany, when the Balkan wars ended with the 1995 Dayton Accords, unsuccessful asylum seekers from the Balkans who lived in Germany received special consideration for work-based immigration.[45]

More recently, Germany has gone beyond language instruction and other traditional integration initiatives by drawing forced migrants into apprenticeships that need new recruits. A new German law in 2023 reflects a similar approach, by replacing successive temporary permits to stay in the country—many held by unsuccessful asylum seekers—with permits that foresee their integration into the labor market.[46]

Responding to forced migration in this way—by allowing some access to work-based admissions—means assigning the private sector an active role in integrating newcomers. The integration that employers and work-based communities can provide is a key aspect of protection that goes beyond immigration status. And this integration fosters respect for the belonging claims of newcomers as they become part of communities in the country.[47]

Another challenge in protection for forced migrants is confronting racial or religious discrimination. All people have a humanity claim to freedom from racial or religious discrimination. But this is a broad statement that's hard to apply. Is it racial or religious discrimination to protect some forced migrants but not others? After Russia invaded Ukraine in 2022, the US government treated Ukrainian forced migrants more generously—through exemptions from the Title 42 border closure and through parole under better terms—than forced migrants from other countries. The EU activated the Temporary Protection Directive for forced migrants from Ukraine, but not from other countries.[48]

Some argue that race or racism explains the better treatment of Ukrainians. Others disagree, citing other reasons such as a geopolitical need to resist Russia, a greater likelihood that protection will be temporary, and geographic proximity in the EU context. My purpose here isn't to resolve this debate. In the United States, the traditional approach of courts to constitutional claims might make it hard to prevail in a racial discrimination lawsuit challenging the favored treatment of Ukraine. Instead, I emphasize that claims of racial and religious discrimination in any approach to protecting forced migrants require close examination.

Engagement with the issue needs to be more serious and honest. Part of the reason is that racism or religious discrimination in protection means that the protection scheme disrespects the humanity claims of forced migrants. But at least as important, though sometimes overlooked, is that racism or religious discrimination in responses to forced migrants also enables and conceals injustice against some insiders who are connected with the disfavored, for example as family members or as employers. Here as elsewhere in responses to human migration, it's tempting but misguided to believe that laws and policies target only people who aren't insiders.

These concerns may have influenced the Biden administration's decision to establish parole programs for Haiti, Cuba, Nicaragua, and Venezuela—though on significantly less favorable terms than for Ukrainians. This wasn't an admission of racism. Geopolitical concerns with left-wing regimes may have been influential or even decisive. But making parole more available in this limited way reflected some sensitivity to the perception of racial discrimination against forced migrants from those countries and insiders close to them.

IN THIS CHAPTER, I've focused on responses by single countries or by the European Union to forced migrants seeking protection. Current policies have arisen and deserve critique in that context. What's missing from this discussion is transnational cooperation—what's often called burden-sharing. But it's hard to talk concretely about burden-sharing without knowing what burdens might be shared—or shifted or shirked. So I've started with issues that single countries typically address: government obstacles to protection, the refugee-migrant line, the nature of protection, individuals versus groups, and discrimination.

Exploring the opportunities and challenges of transnational cooperation with regard to forced migration requires a broader inquiry into transnational cooperation in general. I'll address this after I lay a foundation. Next in this foundation is a fuller discussion of the belonging claims of insiders.

3

Who Can Say That They Belong?

This chapter's focus is the United States, but the lessons have analogues in many other countries. Much of the work in the United States since the 1960s to assess—and sometimes to challenge—immigration laws and policies has emphasized the belonging claims of noncitizens. The argument has been that the government has often not respected their claims as noncitizens who are part of communities in the country.

These advocacy efforts have applied what it's fair to call a *civil rights framework*. The struggle of African Americans to claim their rightful places in American life has supplied many concepts and institutions that make up this framework and have become central to debate in law and politics by guiding claims against racial injustice. This was true whether or not civil rights arguments were successful in any given setting.[1]

In turn, this civil rights framework has been central since the 1960s to efforts to challenge US national borders and immigration policy. As in the civil rights movement, advocates have also sometimes drawn on humanity claims. But the special contribution of the civil rights movement to immigrants and their communities has been an emphasis on belonging claims—on how noncitizens belong to communities in the United States.

In this chapter, I'll unpack how a civil rights framework and an emphasis on the belonging claims of noncitizens became so influential in the United States. This framework has accomplished much to challenge US immigration policy, especially by uncovering racial and religious discrimination, but much of the framework's potential remains untapped. More fundamentally, reliance on belonging claims has some inherent shortcomings and has created political liabilities. A civil rights framework and belonging claims are essential, but I doubt that they alone are enough to make national borders consistent with fairness and justice.

Race in Immigration History

History matters in assessing national borders. In the United States, the emergence of a civil rights framework for challenging immigration has its roots in US history. This framework emerged in the second half of the twentieth century to respond to perceived injustices in immigration and citizenship laws. Some of these injustices reflected racism or were related to racism. The relevant history predates the country's founding.

Slavery in the United States goes back over four centuries to the year 1619. By the mid-1800s, some Black people had gained their freedom as a formal matter, but discrimination in general and citizenship laws in particular remained instruments of subordination. An infamous landmark is the US Supreme Court's 1857 decision in the *Dred Scott* case, which declared that no one of African ancestry born on US territory could be a US citizen.[2]

After the Civil War, in 1868 the Fourteenth Amendment tried to erase the stain of *Dred Scott* by conferring citizenship on anyone born on US soil and "subject to the jurisdiction of the United States." Of course, citizenship alone would not mean full respect for belonging claims; far from it. But this expansion of birthright citizenship was a significant step. And yet, birthright citizenship for the children of Chinese immigrants remained contested in law until 1896. Only gradually did Native Americans gain recognition as birthright citizens—first through treaties with specific tribes, and then for all through a 1924 federal statute.[3]

The acquisition of US citizenship by naturalization was even more restricted by race. A federal statute in 1790 limited eligibility to "free white person[s]." Only in 1870, after the Civil War, did Congress open up naturalization to "aliens of African nativity and to persons of African descent." Immigrants of Asian ancestry remained barred. Congress repealed the last explicit racial barriers to naturalization in 1952.[4]

Alongside this racism in citizenship law, US immigration law expressly used racial bars to keep some people out of the country. One of the earliest federal immigration statutes, enacted in 1875, included a provision that was written as a bar to the admission of prostitutes. But the history of this legislation reveals the law's intent: to keep Chinese women out of the United States, building on an influential strand of public opinion that maligned Chinese women. In 1882, Congress enacted the first of several laws that banned Chinese laborers from the United States. Chinese exclusion remained the law until 1943.[5]

LAWSUITS IN FEDERAL courts challenged several of these anti-Chinese immigration laws as unconstitutional. The US Supreme Court rejected these challenges in several decisions that started a persistent pattern of court deference to immigration decisions by Congress, the president, and executive branch agencies. Lawyers in the United States call this the plenary power doctrine. It severely limits the judicial role when lawsuits challenge the constitutionality of immigration laws or decisions by the US government.[6]

Prominent in several of these Supreme Court decisions in the late 1800s and early 1900s was language that reflected a belief in Anglo-Saxon racial superiority.[7] At other times in this era, racism wasn't as obvious, but just as real. For example, federal, state, and territorial governments treated some newcomers like citizens for many purposes. Noncitizens who wanted to become citizens had to file declarations of intent, sometimes called first papers. As intending citizens, they were often treated like citizens. The federal Homestead Act of 1862 allowed them to settle and acquire land. They could vote in many states and territories. Other federal, state, and local laws treated these noncitizens just like citizens. But only white European newcomers could become intending citizens, given the racial restrictions on naturalization that lasted until the middle of the twentieth century.[8]

THE EMPHASIS ON race and ethnicity continued. In the early twentieth century, many in Congress wanted a federal law to exclude Japanese migrants, but President Theodore Roosevelt resisted. He wanted to minimize any diplomatic affront to Japan, at that time a more substantial international power than China. In 1907, Roosevelt stopped short of outright exclusion but issued a presidential order barring Japanese and Korean immigration to the US mainland from Hawaii, then a US territory. The United States then pressured Japan into the so-called Gentlemen's Agreement. Japan would not issue passports that let Japanese migrants reach the US mainland. In return, the United States agreed to an exception to let Japanese join spouses, children, or parents already in the United States.[9]

A 1917 federal statute went further, blocking immigration from an "Asiatic barred zone." The law generally kept out anyone with ancestry in countries in a zone defined by latitude and longitude from Saudi Arabia eastward, including India, Sri Lanka, Afghanistan, Southeast Asia, Indonesia, and the Asian parts of what would become the Soviet Union. The only exceptions were Japan, already limited by the 1907 Gentlemen's Agreement, and the Philippines as a US colonial possession.[10]

Race soon became even more central to US immigration policy. In the 1920s, Congress adopted the country's first limits on the number of immigrants let in. By that time, congressional leaders were firmly in the grip of the pseudo-science of eugenics, which designated races as biologically superior or inferior. From this perspective, white Europeans weren't necessarily viewed as "white," but instead fell into "Mediterranean," "Alpine," and "Nordic" categories.[11]

Eugenics was the conceptual basis of the national origins system, which first took effect in 1921, followed by a 1924 version that remained central to US immigration law until 1965. This system adopted annual caps on the number of immigrants from any given country. Caps were generous for immigrants from countries in northern and western Europe. Far lower caps limited immigration from southern and eastern Europe, and the system cut off virtually all immigration from Asia and Africa. The goal was to maintain the predominantly white, Anglo-Saxon mix of the US population as it was before large-scale immigration from southern and eastern Europe around the turn of the century.[12]

THE US GOVERNMENT response to Mexican migrants was outwardly different, but it was fundamentally similar in reflecting race as a policy touchstone. Even after federal law started to limit the number of immigrants from the rest of the world, it didn't cap immigration from Mexico or elsewhere in Latin America. That outward difference might have seemed to favor Latin American countries. But the opposite was true. Immigration policy toward Mexico reflected the view that Mexicans were racially inferior to the white, Anglo-Saxon majority in the United States but were a source of needed labor.

This attitude drove Congress' adoption of the Undesirable Aliens Act in 1929, which created the federal crimes of illegal entry and illegal reentry across the physical borders of the United States. Today, these are the most frequently charged crimes in the entire federal system. Its text doesn't target any particular groups by race or ethnicity. But its legislative history makes plain its anti-Mexican purpose: as one member of Congress put it, to prevent the dilution of Anglo-Saxon stock.[13]

This legislation continued the troubled history of relations between the two countries. The Mexican–American War ended in 1848 with the Treaty of Guadalupe-Hidalgo, which forced Mexico to cede over half of its territory, including what is now California, Nevada, Utah, and parts of Colorado, Arizona, New Mexico, and Wyoming. The legacy of conquest included a US labor policy that treated Mexican migrants as a subordinate labor force. Numerous statements by leaders in Congress and the US executive branch made plain their view that Mexicans could be brought to the United States to work, but then sent home when labor needs changed.

Turning to Civil Rights

Given the racial discrimination that had long been central to laws governing immigration and citizenship in the United States, it was only natural
that a civil rights framework would emerge to guide advocacy to assert
the claims of noncitizens. Key legislation marked the shift. Congress
repealed Chinese exclusion in 1943 and racial bars to naturalization in
1952. In 1965, Congress repealed the national origins system and its
explicit advantages for immigrants from northern and western Europe.
The 1965 Immigration Act was a transformational development, driven
by the same civil rights coalition that won the 1964 Civil Rights Act and
the 1965 Voting Rights Act. This cluster of laws reflected a social movement toward racial equality not just domestically, but also in deciding
who could come to the United States.[14]

In the decades that followed, the makeup of the US population
changed profoundly. The foreign-born share rose from under 5 percent in 1970 to almost 14 percent in 2022. Many fewer immigrants
came from Europe, and many more from Asia and Latin America.[15]
It became natural to debate how racial justice issues so central to the
civil rights movement would affect noncitizens. Consider employment
discrimination, affirmative action, and due process.

Many noncitizens saw themselves as marginalized in some of the same
ways as African Americans. It became intuitive to articulate claims in
civil rights terms, often as a matter of impermissible discrimination. But
could noncitizens—or some noncitizens—actually win better treatment
by asserting belonging claims? Answers would come from a series of US
Supreme Court decisions. They are important for the legal rules that
they established, but even more because they were key to the emergence
of a civil rights framework to challenge US laws and policies affecting
immigration and noncitizens.

AN EARLY LANDMARK was the 1971 US Supreme Court decision
in *Graham* v. *Richardson*. This case combined lawsuits against the
states of Arizona and Pennsylvania by several lawful permanent

residents—noncitizens admitted for an indefinite stay and generally eligible for citizenship after five years. Only US citizens were eligible for Arizona and Pennsylvania state welfare payments, and the noncitizens in these cases alleged that this discrimination violated the US Constitution. The Arizona lawsuit included another claim: that because the ineligible noncitizens were "predominantly Mexican nationals the discrimination is also based on race and color."[16]

In *Graham*, the Supreme Court struck down the statutes as unconstitutional, explaining that lawful permanent residents of the United States are a "discrete and insular minority" that the Constitution protects from government discrimination. The Court's emphasis on lawful permanent resident status confirms that the decision recognized their belonging claims. The Court seemed to say that the government can treat citizens better than lawful permanent residents, but only if the difference withstands what lawyers call "strict scrutiny." The difference must serve a "compelling government interest" in the least onerous way. This was the sort of judicial inquiry that had become typical of court decisions involving allegations of racial discrimination.[17]

By the mid-1970s, lawyers were routinely deploying antidiscrimination tools and other civil rights concepts to challenge government decisions to treat lawful permanent residents less well than citizens. These challenges were presented as claims of discrimination based on immigration or citizenship status.[18] Fundamentally, these were challenges based on belonging claims—that noncitizens deserved better treatment because they were part of communities in the United States.

IN THE 1970S, the undocumented population of the United States started to increase sharply. The reasons go back to the 1960's, when US immigration law capped the number of immigrants from Western hemisphere countries for the first time. The same period saw the end of the Bracero program, which had let hundreds of thousands of Mexican farmworkers into the United States to work temporarily. These changes restricted lawful admission but left intact migration patterns that had become deeply engrained for migrants, their communities, and many employers.[19]

I should pause to explain my use of the word "undocumented." I realize that the word "unauthorized," which I've used in prior writing, may be a more neutral term. And many people without lawful status have documents of some sort. But I use undocumented because that seems to be the preference among people without lawful status. A big part of respect for people is deferring to what they prefer to be called. The words "unauthorized" or "illegal" may be suitable when referring to migration or status, but not when talking about people.

Advocates for the undocumented turned to the civil rights framework that had gained traction in *Graham*. Many of these noncitizens believed that they were open to exploitation and discrimination as the victims of US immigration and labor policies that had created a largely nonwhite population of millions without papers. Civil rights arguments on their behalf were a natural fit.

THIS EFFORT TO view undocumented noncitizens in civil rights terms reached a high-water mark in *Plyler* v. *Doe*, a US Supreme Court decision in 1982.[20] The state of Texas adopted a law with the practical effect of keeping undocumented children out of public schools. Several court challenges followed, intentionally modeled after the fight to end school segregation that had prevailed in the Supreme Court almost thirty years earlier in *Brown* v. *Board of Education*. According to the challengers, the Texas law violated the US Constitution by discriminating against both undocumented children and Mexican Americans.

The Supreme Court invalidated the Texas law as unconstitutional discrimination against the children.[21] More precisely, in the context of K-12 public education the children could claim equal protection of the laws under the Fourteenth Amendment to the US Constitution.[22] The Court's analysis made clear that it viewed the children as part of the country's future. In this way, the Court saw the children as asserting belonging claims.

The Court in *Plyler* stopped short of the strict scrutiny that had seemed to decide *Graham*. Instead, it examined Texas' justifications for the statute under a less probing but still meaningful standard that lawyers call "intermediate scrutiny." But crucially, the Court broadened application of a civil rights framework from the lawful permanent residents in *Graham* to the undocumented children in *Plyler*. More subtle but just as significant is that the Court did not take an easier way out. It could have ruled that federal law preempted the Texas law—in other words, that federal immigration laws left the states no room to rely on immigration status to limit a child's education. But the Court addressed the individual rights of undocumented children instead.

Though *Graham* and *Plyler* were milestones, a civil rights framework for analysis and advocacy hasn't always succeeded on behalf of lawful permanent residents or the undocumented. The Supreme Court stepped back from the judicial oversight that *Graham* had seemed to promise.[23] No court has applied the reasoning in *Plyler* to undocumented noncitizens outside of K-12 public education. In 2022, the governor of Texas signaled his readiness to ask the US Supreme Court to overrule *Plyler*.[24] Civil rights arguments often fell short in lawsuits and in campaigns to influence public opinion. And yet the rhetoric of civil rights based on belonging claims became the language of advocacy.

GRAHAM AND PLYLER were direct challenges to laws that disadvantaged some noncitizens. Distinct but related advocacy challenged government treatment of noncitizens as inconsistent with fair procedures for making decisions.[25] In the language of civil rights, this was a matter of due process and the rule of law—which in turn required a fair opportunity to be heard, reasoned decision-making, transparency, and uniformity.

The 1982 US Supreme Court decision in *Landon* v. *Plasencia* is an example of a successful belonging claim based on inadequate process. This case involved a lawful permanent resident of the United States who had been living in Los Angeles with her US citizen spouse and their children. Upon her return from a short trip to Mexico, the US government accused her of bringing back someone who was trying to enter the

United States unlawfully. The government denied her entry and scheduled a hearing, but Maria Plasencia believed that she wasn't getting a fair chance to tell her side of the story.[26]

The Court held that a lawful permanent resident in this setting could claim procedural protections based on due process. In so holding, the Court emphasized that Plasencia had been a lawful permanent resident for years and had immediate family that included US citizens. This reasoning—based on Plasencia's belonging claim—was consistent with the approach to fair decision-making that was central to the civil rights movement.[27]

Defining Insiders

The US Supreme Court was right in *Graham* and *Plasencia* to view lawful permanent residents as insiders. Lawful permanent residents are part of communities in the United States. Countless federal, state, and local laws assume this by treating them almost the same as citizens. They can live in the United States indefinitely unless they become deportable. They can lose their status, but only due to an extended absence, a criminal record of a certain seriousness, or a limited set of other circumstances. Otherwise, they may (but need not) become citizens after five years, or after three years of marriage to a US citizen.

What about noncitizens with permission to live and work in the United States, but not indefinitely? Are they insiders? Some noncitizens have a lawful status as temporary workers or students, or Temporary Protected Status (TPS) for noncitizens from countries beset by dire conditions. Other noncitizens hold an in-between status that reflects US government permission to stay and work. These statuses include parole and Deferred Action for Childhood Arrivals (DACA). As of 2023, about 2 million people had an in-between status under US law. Many are part of communities in the United States, and so are insiders.[28]

ARE UNDOCUMENTED NONCITIZENS also insiders? Because they lack lawful status, the notion that they can be insiders can prompt skepticism. Yet many have strong cases for recognition as insiders. The unauthorized population of the United States is about 11 million people. A high percentage of them work. Virtually all pay federal, state, and local taxes directly—or indirectly in rent or sales taxes. Many are integrated into communities, often with children and other close relatives who are US citizens by birth or naturalization. Many of the undocumented have lived in the United States for a considerable period of years, often a decade or much longer.

I recognize that some may reject my approach to defining insiders—as people who are part of communities in the country, and who therefore can have persuasive belonging claims. A possible objection might be that I offer no precise definition of undocumented insider. That's true. I believe it matters how long someone has lived in the country, but how long is enough is up for debate. Others might object that the notion of insiders assumes some assimilation to mainstream or majority society. But that's not part of the concept of insiders. It's enough to be part of communities in the country. It doesn't matter which communities. A third objection might be that the undocumented hurt US workers and cost the public more than they pay in taxes. These arguments go to whether the undocumented should be here, or whether their belonging claims are persuasive—but they don't refute the connections that make them insiders.

More fundamentally, I'm not trying to define insider precisely. Rather, I want to emphasize two points. One is the concept of the insider and that it's essential to have a robust conversation about who is an insider and who is not. The conversation can include immigration status, but it needs to be much broader. The other point is that insiders have belonging claims, and that it's essential to assess when those claims are persuasive and when they are not. The absence of these conversations is one way that people talk past each other when they try to talk about immigration policy.

The Interests of Insiders

One problem with immigration policy—not just in the United States—is a cramped approach to deciding who counts as insiders. A separate problem is the failure to assess how decisions about immigration affect US citizens. This is a flaw in US immigration law, as a few examples show.

A 2015 decision, *Kerry* v. *Din*, may be the US Supreme Court decision that has gone the furthest in recognizing a US citizen's interests in an immigration case.[29] In *Din*, a majority of the justices took seriously the idea that Fauzia Din, a US citizen, had some claim to fair procedures in her efforts to secure permission for her Afghan husband to join her in the United States. But the federal government prevailed because the Court found that the procedures that the federal government actually provided Din were what the Constitution required.

Any recognition in *Din* of effects on a US citizen had little influence on the US Supreme Court's 2018 decision in *Trump v. Hawaii*. The Court upheld the Trump administration's ban on people from six majority-Muslim countries who wanted to come to the United States to become lawful permanent residents. A majority of justices let national security concerns override substantial evidence that the president was keeping his campaign promise to bar Muslims. The Court's analysis considered only injury to the banned outsiders, putting little weight on the interests of citizens, lawful permanent residents, religious communities, companies, and universities who suffered because of the ban.[30]

In 2024, the U.S. Supreme Court extended the *Hawaii* approach when it decided *Department of State v. Muñoz*.[31] The case involved Sandra Muñoz, a US citizen who had petitioned for her husband to become a lawful permanent resident based on their marriage. When a consular officer denied her husband's visa application, she wanted to know why. According to Muñoz, the federal government wouldn't give her enough information to allow her to contest its decision. This, she argued, violated her constitutional right to due process. But the Court's scrutiny was limited. It ruled against Muñoz, minimizing the legal relevance of any injury to her as an affected citizen. The Court found that Muñoz's right to marriage did not include a right to live with her spouse in the United States.

It's possible to see *Din*, *Hawaii*, and *Muñoz* as decisions that took the interests of citizens seriously. But I'm not persuaded. Telling is that these court decisions relied on the plenary power doctrine to avoid serious examination of constitutional challenges to the federal government's immigration decisions. Serious analysis won't always mean that the challengers win. But looking closely at constitutional challenges would be a sign of respect for insiders whose voices are now muted or silenced.

In these three decisions and others that are similar, the Supreme Court elevated the interests of some insiders over the interests of others. It preferred insiders who had no ties with the noncitizens that the government was keeping out. The Court disadvantaged insiders with ties to those noncitizens. This unequal treatment of insiders with these ties was a profound failure.[32]

The Limits of National Belonging

Suppose that more people in the United States were to be recognized as insiders with belonging claims, thus as people who deserve more recognition and respect. Put differently, suppose that decision-makers took more seriously how national borders affect insiders. Differences in treatment would then draw more scrutiny than is now typical. Belonging claims might tap more of their potential to improve national borders. This might happen in similar ways in other countries—each with its own versions of the belonging claims of insiders.

But migration patterns have changed worldwide in the past few decades. To be sure, the treatment of insiders within national borders remains contested, especially for people with an in-between status or no lawful status at all. But the role of immigration in the political arenas of many countries has shifted and expanded. Immigration and the physical border have become central to politics—perhaps even the epicenter.[33] In the United States, the presidential campaigns of Donald

Trump insisted that the border was out of control, and that control had to be regained before America could become "great again." Similar political dynamics explain the rise of anti-immigrant movements in many countries.

This means that the most heated immigration controversies involve migrants with more attenuated personal ties to the countries that they reach. I recognize that the migrants' countries of origin and their destination countries may have historical ties. But these migrants are typically not insiders in destination countries.

With large numbers of new arrivals, claims based on national belonging can sound off-key, lose traction, and create political openings for demagogues who trade on hostility toward newcomers. Texas Governor Greg Abbott said about President Biden: "He does not care about Americans. He cares more about people who are not from this country."[34] President Trump tweeted about border crossers: "We cannot allow all of these people to invade our Country." Many of these comments are racially inflected, such as Trump's disparaging comments about Haiti and other "shithole" countries.[35]

The vital lesson is that claims based on national belonging can't do all of the work, even if some new arrivals have family or other ties with insiders. As a path toward better borders, it's inadequate to assert belonging claims without also understanding how belonging claims and humanity claims can work together.

PART II

Admission, Exclusion, and Time

4

Who Should Get In, or Be Kept Out?

What should shape decisions to let in some newcomers and keep others out? This is the central question for this chapter. I won't propose specific prescriptions about numbers—about how many people should be let in or be kept out, nor about some specific categories to let in and keep out. Instead, as in other chapters, I'll set out a way of thinking about these decisions consistent with respect for the humanity claims of all affected people and the belonging claims of insiders.

Families

Family ties are central to the rules for admitting immigrants in many countries around the world. The idea is to let people live their lives as part of families. A central example is letting people who are already residents of a country have a spouse and other close relatives come to join them, so they can live together. Why is this true?[1]

A big reason is a belief that family ties are fundamental to human flourishing. Close units of people related by blood, marriage, or adoption share their lives in intimate ways that help everyone in the family thrive. Strong societies nurture these ties, to benefit not only family members, but also society as a whole. These views explain why admissions schemes often take for granted the value of fostering family.

For a closer look, my analysis focuses on the United States, though similar issues arise in many countries. Family-based categories let in more newcomers than any other categories for long-term admission as lawful permanent residents. The relatives who qualify most easily are "immediate relatives." This includes the spouses and children of US citizens, as well as the parents of citizens who are at least twenty-one years old. In defining "spouse," same-sex marriages count, reflecting the right to marry under the US Constitution. "Children" are offspring who are unmarried and under twenty-one, including many (but not all) stepchildren, adopted children, and children born out of wedlock. US law doesn't cap how many immediate relatives may become lawful permanent residents, so there is no official backlog, but paperwork can take months or years.[2]

US law also lets other relatives become lawful permanent residents. Sons and daughters of citizens, spouses and unmarried sons and daughters of lawful permanent residents, and siblings of adult citizens can all qualify. Each year, only a limited number of noncitizens in these categories may become lawful permanent residents. No category includes grandparents and grandchildren. Waiting periods are a core aspect of this system. They can be long, and even longer for some countries due to caps on the number of immigrants from any given country in many of the family categories.[3]

A few aspects of US immigration law recognize family ties in other ways. When newcomers are admitted, their spouses and unmarried minor children can generally accompany or follow them. Family ties can also matter when noncitizens might otherwise be barred from admission, for example because of a criminal conviction. In such cases, close relatives of citizens or lawful permanent residents may be eligible for a waiver. Family ties can also matter in shielding noncitizens from deportation.[4]

HUMANITY CLAIMS AND belonging claims typically combine to suggest what family ties should count. Given the central role of family life in human flourishing, people have persuasive humanity claims to live with close family members. Belonging claims also arise in this setting, based on the same notion of family life. What, then, is the connection between humanity claims and belonging claims in the context of immigration based on family ties?

Respecting family life in a destination country with a spouse and unmarried minor children can be a persuasive focus for both a humanity claim and a belonging claim. The humanity claim means that immigrants who are being let into a country should be able to bring with them their spouse and unmarried minor children. The belonging claim means that insiders in the destination country should be able to have their spouse and unmarried minor children immigrate across a national border to join them and live together in the destination country.

This reasoning supports both a humanity claim and a belonging claim to immigrate to the United States based on a same-sex marriage. The humanity claim would be based on the idea that family unity should extend to same-sex marriages. The belonging claim would have a related but distinct and firmer basis: the US Supreme Court's affirmation of the constitutional guarantee that same-sex couples have the same right to marry as everyone else. To deny the insider a life in the United States with a same-sex spouse would be to treat this insider worse than other insiders.

WHAT ABOUT LONG waits for immigration based on family ties? The waiting lists for the limited number of slots are so long that in the recent past, people have had to wait over five years to join their lawful permanent resident spouses in the United States. One way to respect both humanity claims and belonging claims is to increase the number of available immigration slots for at least the spouses and unmarried minor children of lawful permanent residents.

Another way to respect both humanity claims and belonging claims is interim entry permission for noncitizens who have qualified in an immigration category but are waiting for a family-based immigration slot to become available. In 2023, the Biden administration announced a program to make this possible by granting parole to let in qualifying relatives from El Salvador, Columbia, Guatemala, and Honduras. Instead of waiting in their home countries, they can come to the United States to join their family member while they wait for the backlog to clear so they can become lawful permanent residents.[5]

What about siblings? Some observers might think that immigration laws can limit migration on the basis of sibling relationships without disrespecting humanity claims. But it's hard to say this confidently. Some siblings may be much like parents or other relatives. A related issue has arisen in US law. An earlier federal statute allowed a noncitizen to avoid deportation based on extreme hardship to a spouse, parent, or child who was a citizen or lawful permanent resident. Attorneys for one such noncitizen argued that the statute allowed recognition of extreme hardship to someone if they were the "functional equivalent" of a spouse, parent, or child. In a case involving a niece and her aunt, the US Supreme Court rejected this argument, emphasizing that the statute's text specified no relationships other than spouse, parent, or child.[6]

But respect for the belonging claims of insiders might suggest the opposite result. From this perspective, what matters is the substance of the relationship, not formal recognition in family law. That said, this reasoning has its limits. First, how many newcomers would this reasoning let in? A large number might be functional equivalents of specified relatives. Would the overall number exceed what can be adopted and sustained politically? And is it a higher priority to test political limits in this area of immigration policy than in others?

It may help to mention how US immigration law treats children who are adopted under the age of sixteen. The relationship between adoptive child and parent is the same for immigration purposes as the relationship between biological child and parent. At the same time, the adoption ends legal recognition of the biological parent-child relationship.[7] Treating other immigration settings in this way would mean that the citizen or lawful permanent resident could ask for recognition of a functionally equivalent relationship, which could then displace recognition of the preexisting relationship.

This approach may still run into political limits on numbers. It also raises questions about how to assess what should count as a functional equivalent. The process of evaluating closeness might intrude on privacy or leave too much discretion to government officials. As for numbers, what about letting citizens and lawful permanent residents sponsor a very limited number of people based on any very close relationship?

WHY HAS THIS discussion of family ties seemed to assume so far that only citizens and lawful permanent residents are insiders? Being an insider involves much more than legal status. Undocumented people typically belong to communities in the country, so they can be insiders with persuasive belonging claims. All insider claims deserve to be taken seriously. Doing so would be a big change from current practice.

Not all insider claims are equally persuasive, however. Strong justifications can allow differential treatment.[8] What justifications are strong enough? Should only citizens and lawful permanent residents be able to sponsor noncitizens to immigrate to join them? Should citizens be able to sponsor a broader set of relatives than lawful permanent residents can? Why should undocumented people be able to sponsor anyone?

The best responses would direct attention to the need to offer lawful status to many undocumented people. I'll say more about this in a later chapter. For now, my point is that rather than allowing undocumented people as such to sponsor relatives, it would be more coherent to make sure that immigration status matches someone's connection to communities in the country. For example, if people lack lawful status because of a labor policy that has unfairly marginalized them as without lawful status, then the most sensible remedy is conferring lawful status—which in turn can allow immigration based on family ties.[9]

For lawful permanent residents, spouses and unmarried minor children are such close relatives that humanity claims and belonging claims should make family unity automatic and immediate. As for other relationships, the focus should be on how lawful permanent residents can become citizens. If the naturalization process is routine and nondiscriminatory, then it may be justified to give citizens greater opportunities for family unity than lawful permanent residents have.

Workers and Investors

Who should be let in to work? How does this compare to immigration based on family ties? One key consideration is that the contrast between work-based and family-based immigration isn't as stark as it might seem. Work and family are related. Family ties can be vital for the economic well-being of families, communities, and the economy as a whole. Parents and grandparents often care for children so other family members can work. Relatives can co-sign for loans, connect newcomers with jobs, and help navigate red tape. Participating in the economy through work and other forms of engagement can be essential for well-being in a family. In short, analyzing economic contributions means seeing immigrants in more than just economic terms.[10]

It's still worth looking at the aspects of immigration that are most closely related to work and other economic participation, including self-employment. As with family ties, how might the arrival of immigrants affect insiders who might have belonging claims? For example, some insiders might be part of enterprises that want to employ immigrants, or they might benefit from immigration in less direct ways.

Immigrants can create new jobs and keep businesses afloat so that other workers can stay employed. The reason is that many immigrants complement—and don't replace—the existing workforce. Immigrants help expand the economy by increasing both demand and supply. Without new workers, employers might raise prices, relocate outside the country, or go out of business. Immigrant contributions to innovation have been massive. The COVID-19 pandemic showed that in jobs where remote work was impossible, immigrants were essential in healthcare, childcare, nursing homes, agriculture, food service, retail stores, and more.[11]

Skeptical insiders might feel that their economic situation will suffer because of newcomers in the workforce. These insiders also deserve respect for their belonging claims. The challenge is taking these concerns seriously without letting them become insurmountable barriers to positive infusions of labor and talent. I'll devote all of a later chapter to this important topic.[12]

FOR THE BELONGING claims of insiders who favor more noncitizens in the workforce, the problem is an admission scheme that is quite restrictive compared to the economy's need for workers. In the United States, qualifying categories generally require a high level of formal education, usually at least a four-year college degree. Noncitizens who meet this minimum but don't have advanced degrees have to wait in long lines.

Many potential immigrants in the work-based categories must navigate a complex bureaucratic process that's designed to see if they will displace US workers or accept lower wages or worse working conditions. The consensus is that this requirement has only modest value in evaluating harm to US workers. Some evidence even suggests that it operates with a skew against workers from some regions of the world.[13]

In the United States, the work-based categories for becoming lawful permanent residents are limited to 140,000 immigrants each year. But this number exaggerates how many are actually workers. More than half of immigrants in work-based categories are not the workers themselves, but instead their spouses and unmarried minor children. As in the family-based categories, annual caps force many who qualify to wait a long time—often years—before becoming lawful permanent residents. This reflects not just the overall limit for the work-based categories, but also the limits on the number of immigrants from any given country.[14]

The mismatch between strong demand for workers and restrictive admissions is no better for workers who come in nonimmigrant categories. This is the official terminology for coming to the United States lawfully for a limited time period to work, typically in a particular job for a particular employer. One major category—H-1B temporary workers—has an annual cap. The federal government distributes visas by lottery to employers who apply for the limited number that are available each year.[15]

Because lawful work-based admissions are so limited but the economy's workforce needs are so pressing, millions of people work without papers, with some degree of government tolerance, acquiescence, or invitation. Some work in the cash economy. Others are in a broader array of jobs using false documents for identity and work authorization. Many have been in the United States for years. As these undocumented workers become a part of communities in the United States, they become insiders with persuasive belonging claims against any exploitation through precarious jobs, wage theft, dangerous working conditions, squalid housing, and worse.[16] Looking at this population from the perspective that belonging claims deserve respect, the priority in the short term is legalization to offer durable lawful status with a path to citizenship. I'll say more about this in a later chapter. Along with legalization, long-term reform requires expansion of work-based admissions combined with measures to share the prosperity that immigration generates.[17]

WORK-BASED IMMIGRATION IS related to programs that allow immigration based on financial investment. Like work-based immigration, investment-based immigration can help the destination country's economy grow, including through job creation. For example, the United States accepts new lawful permanent residents if they invest a considerable sum of money in certain types of projects. The minimum amount depends on the geographical area. Other countries also offer investors a durable residence status and even citizenship.[18]

These programs have prompted some skepticism and opposition. For some critics, it's troubling to admit people based on wealth. Another objection is that admissions programs for investors may not bring the economic benefits that supporters tout. A related concern is that investor programs focus on short-term gains, and that immigrants in employment-based categories might make more meaningful contributions in the long run. Critics also point to the potential for fraud on investors, communities, and governments.[19]

From the perspective of humanity claims and belonging claims, investment programs could be unobjectionable, but it depends on how they are set up and operate. I've just mentioned some potential problems. Other risks call for vigilance. For example, many investment programs involve the construction of hotel complexes. If the project exposes workers to exploitative or dangerous conditions, it may disrespect the humanity claims and the belonging claims of the workers and their families and communities. Investment-based admissions should not allow some insiders to gain an advantage over other insiders by providing a vehicle for financial exploitation.

As with family-based and work-based admissions, my purpose here is to ask how investment-based admissions might implicate humanity claims and belonging claims as policymakers make choices that are contested politically. My questions don't yield detailed constraints, requirements, or numbers, but they identify some risks and suggest some guardrails.

Who Is Kept Out?

Under US law, qualifying in a category that allows admission is just the first step toward becoming a lawful permanent resident. Noncitizens must also not be "inadmissible." For example, marriage to a citizen qualifies noncitizens for an admission category, but the federal immigration statute might block them for a past criminal conviction, affiliation with a "terrorist organization," insufficient financial means, or past deportation from the country. Orders and policies of the federal executive branch can have similar effects. The Trump administration's ban on immigrants from six majority-Muslim countries is a prime example.[20]

Drafting and applying these laws are complex tasks. What prior crimes should keep someone out? What is a "terrorist organization"? When are financial means insufficient? Are waivers available in individual cases? What is the process for applying these rules? The basic question is whether inadmissibility grounds and their application are consistent or inconsistent with respect for humanity claims and belonging claims.

It's hard to say categorically how any given inadmissibility ground might fare when it is actually drafted and applied. As an example, consider a law that bars people from a country if they want to overthrow the destination country's government. This law sounds like it might be unobjectionable, but it's not so simple. This law might be a cover for other types of discrimination. The government might administer it in a way that bars people selectively or bars people not at all within its scope.

In deciding if this law and its application should be part of a country's response to migration, it's essential to ask first about respecting humanity claims. For instance, does it deny protection to a forced migrant who qualifies as a refugee by putting an unreasonable burden on them to prove that they also are not a threat to national security? Second, does the law too casually or too categorically reject the persuasive belonging claims of an insider to have a spouse immigrate to start family life together?

Exclusion on the basis of race or religion almost certainly disrespects the humanity claims of anyone affected and the belonging claims of insiders. Other cases are harder. I'm not making categorical prescriptions about laws that bar noncitizens from a country. Instead, what matters is that the conversation about any law or policy assess it in terms of humanity claims and belonging claims.

For the belonging claims of insiders, a touchstone is whether the inadmissibility ground rests on a difference in treatment that would be intolerable in a context not involving immigration and national borders. But the plenary power doctrine in US immigration law insulates the federal government's immigration decisions from this essential inquiry by courts. For example, the US Supreme Court didn't seriously evaluate whether the Trump ban on immigration from six majority-Muslim countries was religious discrimination that disrespected the belonging claims of insiders and humanity claims of all.[21]

From Where?

How does respect for humanity claims and belonging claims matter for selecting or excluding based on a noncitizen's country of origin? From the 1920s to 1965, US immigration law limited the number of immigrants based on where they came from. The system's purpose was to preserve the racial and ethnic composition of the United States as it was in the late 1800s by favoring immigration from northern and west-ern Europe. It allowed some immigrants from southern and eastern Europe, but from any country in Asia and Africa the limit was about 100 each year. By discriminating on the basis of race and ethnicity, this system reflected bias that disrespected humanity claims and belonging claims.

In the 1960s, the United States adopted a new system with a uniform annual limit—now about 25,400—on the number of new lawful per-manent residents born in any one country of origin. These caps apply to the work and family categories, but not to immediate relatives. Applying the same per-country limit to all countries regardless of population or demand for immigrant visas has led to especially severe backlogs of years for many family and work-based immigrants from Mexico, China, India, and the Philippines.[22]

Another aspect of US law—the annual diversity lottery—also relies on someone's country of origin to distribute admission slots among coun-tries. Congress adopted several versions of the lottery starting in 1989 as a partial offset to the end of US immigration law's historical preference for immigrants from northern and western Europe. An early version reserved 40 percent of visas for the Irish. But the lottery's principal effect has been to increase immigration from countries, especially in Africa, from which few immigrants had come previously. Noncitizens from "high-admission" countries are not eligible.[23]

Both per-country limits and the diversity lottery apply numerical caps based on a noncitizen's country of origin. This means that the US system treats countries equally, but it treats people unequally. The insiders who would favor the arrival of these immigrants are also treated differently, whenever an immigrant's country of birth forces a relative or employee from that country to wait longer.

SO UNDERSTOOD, THESE caps call for strong justifications. Do connec-tions between countries of origin and destination countries based on history, geography, or economics argue convincingly against a uniform annual cap on the number of new lawful permanent residents from a specific country? These broader contexts may suggest an increase in the number of new immigrants from some countries, but it's hard to see how it justifies a lower limit on admissions based on country of origin.[24]

One justification for limiting the number of immigrants from any given country might be to promote diversity among immigrants as a whole and thus in the destination country. Is this reasoning persuasive? It depends on how per-country caps balance progress toward this goal against the hardships that long waits can cause. For example, eliminating per-country caps or raising them to reflect country population or historical ties could shorten waits without skewing the overall mix of immigrants in a way that undermines diversity to a troubling degree. This assessment depends heavily on whether the total number of immigrants admitted is constant or increases.

Numbers, Integration, and the Undocumented

What about the overall number of immigrants let into a destination country? Is this a matter of "capacity"? And what does capacity mean? Two important perspectives on these issues come from assessing immigrant integration and the unauthorized population.

Integration is vital for ensuring that newcomers, as they become part of communities in a country, have their belonging claims respected. Integration is also vital for the civic solidarity that is needed for a strong society in any country. This reasoning suggests that the number of immigrants must be low enough to allow integration that's respectful and effective—not necessarily immediately, but as measured over a generation or two.

That said, integration isn't just about numbers. More crucial in determining capacity to integrate is a destination country's approach to integration. If integration is begrudging or coercive, or has scant fiscal support, or if laws and policies don't actively foster integration as a basic policy goal, then capacity will seem more limited than it really is. Fewer newcomers will seem to be "too many."

Immigration categories also influence whether integration is effective. For instance, fostering family unity in admissions is likely to foster integration. Many sorts of family ties can matter, but children are especially important. The children of immigrants do much to help their parents integrate. Children often navigate for parents, who may find the ways of a new land bewildering. More fundamentally, children prompt families to look ahead to future generations, and to feel connections and commitments to their new country more strongly than they might from the perspective of the parents' generation alone.

WHEN MEASURING HOW many people are let into a country, it's tempting to disregard people without lawful immigration status. But doing so distorts assessment of numbers and capacity. One key point is that many undocumented people become part of communities in the country, but their lack of status hampers their integration. This means that a large and less integrated unauthorized population will make capacity seem more limited than if the undocumented noncitizens who have become insiders are able to acquire lawful status.

The same connection between immigration status and capacity appears in assessing noncitizens who are in a temporary immigration status. Many don't become part of communities in the country, but some do. If they don't integrate, then just like the undocumented they will make capacity seem more limited than it might be with policies that integrate them more effectively, as newcomers who at first seem temporary become insiders over time. This brings me to the next chapter, which explores what it means to come to a country temporarily or on a more indefinite basis.

5

Should Newcomers Stay Temporarily or Indefinitely?

A basic question about newcomers probes expectations about time. Are newcomers in a country temporarily, or is their stay indefinite? I'll use the word "indefinite" rather than "permanent" because it more accurately captures the notion that there is no prescribed end to their stay. This is true even if they have a durable immigration status, such as lawful permanent resident of the United States.

The contrast between the temporary and the indefinite arises with admissions of all types. Why one or the other? Who chooses, and when? Labeling newcomers as temporary also prompts asking: Will it really be temporary, or is it indefinite? This chapter explains that if borders are to respect belonging claims, borders must give newcomers—even if let in temporarily at first—some option to stay indefinitely if they become insiders. Nothing is necessarily self-contradictory or deceptive about coming temporarily and staying indefinitely.

Temporary Statuses

Many countries admit some newcomers on a temporary basis. For example, the United States has "nonimmigrant" statuses for workers, students, business people, artists, athletes, entertainers, tourists, and others. Several categories of temporary workers have specific requirements for the work and the worker. The H-1B category is generally for people with a four-year college degree or equivalent. The H-2A category is for agricultural workers. The H-2B category is for temporary workers in other occupations or industries. Rules for each category set wage minimums and otherwise address concerns that newcomers might undercut the wages and working conditions that employers offer to citizens and lawful permanent residents.[1]

Closely related are nonimmigrant categories for business settings. L-1 nonimmigrants must be employees coming to work in the United States after having worked at least one year for the same employer outside the country. The E-1 and E-2 categories implement international treaties that provide for the admission of traders, investors, and key employees of companies engaged in trading or investment.[2]

What matters for this discussion are the basic features of these categories in many countries, not the specifics that vary within or across countries. In general, nonimmigrant status is tied to a specific activity in which nonimmigrants must remain engaged. They usually may stay only for a set period of time, though extensions are possible in many categories. By way of exception, students in the United States may stay as long as they continue to study where they said they would.[3]

These traditional nonimmigrant statuses don't cover all of the many people whom a government recognizes as lawfully present. In the United States, examples include parole, Temporary Protected Status (TPS), and Deferred Action for Childhood Arrivals (DACA). People in these categories have limited permission to stay and typically may work. These categories are sometimes called twilight or liminal statuses, but I'll use the label "in-between" because it's more accurate even if it's less vivid and a bit clunky. Like traditional nonimmigrant statuses, these in-between statuses don't allow indefinite residence. As of 2023, almost 2 million noncitizens in the United States were in some type of in-between status.[4]

In-between Statuses

Parole is an in-between status that lets noncitizens enter or stay in the United States for a period of time that's limited but often renewable. Unlike nonimmigrant status, parole isn't formal admission. But noncitizens with parole aren't undocumented, and they typically may work.

A federal statute authorizes parole for "urgent humanitarian reasons or significant public benefit."[5] Over the years, Congress has revised the statute several times to try to limit the use of parole, but multiple presidents managed to preserve enough latitude to use parole selectively as an alternative to admission. The government sometimes uses parole to let noncitizens enter for medical care or other humanitarian reasons, or while their applications for lawful permanent residence are being processed. Significantly, the US government has used parole to let forced migrants into the United States.[6]

Parole for forced migrants began in 1956, soon after the Soviet Union put down an uprising in Hungary. The Eisenhower administration came under significant pressure to protect Hungarians, whom many viewed as refugees, but no more visas were available that year to allow formal admission. President Eisenhower made what was then innovative use of parole to let about 30,000 Hungarians enter the United States.

Almost every presidential administration since Eisenhower has used parole to let some forced migrants enter the United States when other pathways weren't available. Parole was instrumental in receiving Cubans over several decades, starting in 1959 after the Cuban Revolution. In the 1970s, hundreds of thousands of people leaving Vietnam, Cambodia, and Laos were paroled into the United States.[7]

President Biden used parole starting in 2021 for forced migrants from Afghanistan, then Ukraine, and then Cuba, Haiti, Nicaragua, and Venezuela. These programs were meant to reduce the number of forced migrants traveling to the southern border of the United States, and to allow them to avoid the risks to life and limb on the journey from their own countries. Another Biden program authorized parole for immigrant visa applicants from Colombia, El Salvador, Guatemala, and Honduras.

If they already qualified in a family-based admission category and were waiting for their immigrant visa, they could enter the United States on parole rather than wait in their countries of origin.[8]

US law also provides for Temporary Protected Status, or TPS, for people from countries beset by severe conditions. Like parole, TPS is not formal admission. Instead, it is an in-between status for noncitizens who generally must have been in the United States when the federal government designated their countries for TPS. A detailed 1990 federal statute sets out a process and criteria for designation.[9]

For forced migrants who might not qualify for asylum, TPS is crucial. It avoids the individual determinations where lawyers and other help are practically necessary for individual applications to succeed. The government also saves substantial resources. TPS holders usually may stay in the United States, with permission to work, for an initial eighteen-month period, and often with extensions.[10]

ANOTHER IN-BETWEEN STATUS is Deferred Action for Childhood Arrivals, or DACA. The Obama administration established the DACA program in 2012 for undocumented noncitizens in the United States who first arrived by 2007 and at a young age. DACA authorizes executive branch officials to exercise discretion to grant permission to stay, but it is not formal admission to the United States.

The term of a DACA grant is a renewable two years, with eligibility to work. DACA holders must meet some requirements for education or service in the US military. Criminal convictions of a certain seriousness will disqualify applicants. About 827,000 young people became DACA recipients from the program's inception in 2012 until 2017, when a federal district court issued an order barring new initial DACA grants.[11]

WHEN MIGHT NONCITIZENS in temporary or in-between statuses actually stay indefinitely? This might happen if they hold a temporary or in-between status for such a long time—perhaps even decades—that their stay approaches the practically indefinite. They might lose their status, but remain in the country without status. Or a temporary or in-between status might give noncitizens enough time to move into a category that lets them stay indefinitely, perhaps based on family or work. For example, in the United States about 76,000 DACA recipients had become lawful permanent residents in various immigrant categories by late 2023.

Temporary and in-between statuses show variations along two basic dimensions. First, if noncitizens move into a more durable status, it's accurate to say that their original status was transitional. If they don't move, their status is terminal. Second, temporary and in-between statuses vary from more precarious to less precarious. Nonimmigrant and in-between statuses are all precarious to a degree. In the United States, temporary workers generally lose their nonimmigrant status if they are no longer in the same job. Students must have a minimum course load where they enroll.

In-between statuses are more precarious than temporary nonimmigrant statuses in several ways. In-between statuses generally don't establish the formal admission that might ease transition to lawful permanent residence. In-between statuses are also precarious if the authority to grant them is contested. As far back as the Eisenhower years, the use of parole to let people into the United States has drawn heavy criticism and some court challenges. In 2023, several Republican-led states sued to block the Biden administration's parole programs for Cuba, Haiti, Nicaragua, and Venezuela, claiming that these programs intrude on Congress' power to regulate admission.[12]

TPS has a more specific and detailed statutory basis, but it is precarious because country designations expire unless the federal executive branch renews them. In 2018, the Trump administration announced that TPS for several countries would end. Lawsuits blocked these terminations for the remainder of the Trump administration and first few years of the Biden administration. President Biden later restored the designations, but precarity remains.[13]

DACA is also a precarious status. Its legal foundation is the overall immigration enforcement system and its inherent need to make discretionary choices. But DACA lacks the more specific statutory authorizations that parole and TPS have. This may explain why a federal district court barred new DACA grants, though renewals are allowed.

Beyond precarity in the courts, different administrations have taken different positions on DACA. In 2017, the Trump administration announced that it was rescinding DACA. The US Supreme Court found that the rescission was ineffective because the process to rescind it was flawed. A future presidential administration may rescind it properly. In 2022, the Biden administration issued a regulation to put DACA on firmer legal footing, but the legal basis for that regulation, and thus for DACA itself, remained contested. The issue will likely reach the US Supreme Court.[14]

Beyond this, individual grants of in-between status—such as parole, TPS, and DACA—are precarious in another way. They depend on discretionary decisions by government officials, who may deny an individual grant or renewal, or revoke an individual grant. Disappointed applicants generally can't appeal these decisions.

Reasons for the Temporary and In-between

The next task is to evaluate temporary and in-between statuses. It's essential to understand why these statuses exist. The reasons often combine in the decision-making process, but it's worth understanding how these reasons differ from each other. One reason is that decision-makers may have pragmatic political reasons to defer decisions on these and other immigration issues. In the United States, parole and TPS ease some of the political pressure to decide if more forced migrants should get asylum. DACA has a similar effect by avoiding a stark choice between stiffer enforcement with unbridled discretion on the one hand and legalization and a path to citizenship on the other. Deferring reflects the absence of the resolve and political capital needed to reach a decision. This is unsurprising in immigration policy, given how fraught a wedge issue it is in electoral politics.[15]

From the perspective of the migrants themselves, it may make sense to defer a decision on how long they will stay. They may be uncertain about what they want and apprehensive about life in a new land. They may need time—maybe measured in years—to decide if they want to settle there or return to their country of origin. This is true regardless of why they migrate—to work or to be with family, or because they have no choice. Just as government decision-makers may want to wait before deciding, this is also true for migrants.

Relatedly, suppose a decision-maker wants to increase the number of noncitizens who become lawful permanent residents. This may be more likely to happen in two stages. The first is to admit more temporary workers or allow forced migrants to use TPS or parole. Though these noncitizens' lives may be precarious and stressful, in stage two many will use their time in temporary or in-between statuses to become lawful permanent residents in a category based on work or family.

Even if that doesn't happen for many noncitizens, it may be easier overall to take in more workers or forced migrants gradually. For example, protection may be temporary at first, but decision-makers may decide later to let some forced migrants stay indefinitely. Such approaches may encounter less resistance than striving initially to have more immigrants based on work or expanded protection for forced migrants. This reason is not necessarily rooted in any legislative failure or subterfuge. Especially if decisions must respond to fast-moving events, it can be better to adopt interim measures quickly, and then be more deliberate when considering durable immigration status later.

A RELATED REASON for temporary and in-between statuses is to get more information before letting newcomers stay indefinitely. For temporary workers, this may be facts about the work they do or their long-term potential to contribute to the economy. This information may not be available reliably from the person's background before arrival. Also more available after a period of time following arrival might be evidence that someone is law-abiding, has paid taxes, and so forth. In this way, some decision-makers may view temporary and in-between statuses as probationary periods.[16]

In broader economic perspective, more information will become available about workforce needs. Perhaps an economic sector needs fewer workers than it did when the workers first came. Similar thinking might apply to protecting forced migrants. Even if they don't qualify as refugees, governments may offer them limited protection, in order to respond to the immediate urgency to protect. Many forced migrants who gain temporary protection may hope to return to their country of origin if conditions there improve, and many will return. Deferring a decision on indefinite protection allows more facts to emerge before conferring durable status.

Another reason for temporary or in-between statuses is more troubling. Some influential people or institutions may prefer to have noncitizens in these statuses to keep them more compliant or passive. Some employers may want employees in temporary or in-between statuses as a way to keep their workforce cheap, flexible, and vulnerable.[17] This is especially true if temporary workers must stay in their jobs to keep their immigration status. Similarly, noncitizens with parole or DACA may be more compliant in various aspects of daily life because of the uncertainty that comes with precarious status.

SOME DECISION-MAKERS may view temporary or in-between statuses as alternatives to having noncitizens with no lawful status at all. Many destination countries have very limited work-based pathways to lawful permanent residence or similar durable statuses. This seems especially true for workers with modest or no formal education or training. Some aspects of family-based pathways are also constricted, depending on the relationship and country of origin. Permission to come temporarily gives migrants less reason to come outside the law. Similarly, many people with TPS and DACA in the United States would otherwise be undocumented.

Viewing temporary and in-between statuses as alternatives to being undocumented runs into the objection that another alternative is more vigorous enforcement of immigration laws, including more deportations. Others would suggest a very different option: offering lawful immigration status through a legalization program. I'll explore legalization and enforcement in later chapters.[18]

FROM ANOTHER PERSPECTIVE, temporary and in-between statuses are tools for international economic development and foreign policy.

Noncitizens in temporary and in-between statuses may retain stronger ties to countries of origin than noncitizens who are immigrants admitted indefinitely. This suggests that temporary and in-between statuses are important for enabling migrants to make contributions to their countries of origin.

For example, people in temporary and in-between statuses send money back to their countries of origin. These remittances can buoy the economy by helping to build houses, educate children, start and grow small businesses, and in general by improving the lives of people there. People in temporary and in-between statuses also make contributions beyond money. Contacts with sending communities allow people to impart entrepreneurial know-how, language fluency, occupational skills, and other knowledge, perspectives, and experience. Decision-makers may believe that these features allow temporary and in-between statuses to advance similar goals by supplementing or substituting for direct aid to a migrant's country of origin.[19]

Problems with the Temporary and In-between

Concerns about temporary and in-between statuses deserve airing. Admitting temporary workers exposes them to exploitation by employers. I've already mentioned that some employers may prefer temporary workers for this reason. Immigration policy that creates the conditions for mistreatment of temporary workers disrespects their humanity claims. As they become part of communities in the country, including through work, it disrespects their belonging claims as well.

Disrespect is more likely if a temporary worker's immigration status depends on staying in the same job for the same employer. Workers who can't change jobs lose a key way to escape unsafe workplace conditions, wage theft, or other abusive treatment. Many workers are burdened by onerous debts owed to employers and recruiters, don't get paid for work performed, or don't have access to medical care for on-the-job injuries. Many live in squalid housing. Some employers take away identification documents and threaten to call immigration authorities if workers make trouble.[20] Governments of the workers' countries of origin might not have the desire or ability to protect their citizens in other countries.

The remedy is not to stop temporary admissions for work, but instead to enforce workplace laws that protect newcomers, no matter whether newcomers are let in or allowed to stay temporarily or indefinitely. It is crucial to keep employers from invoking the threat of government enforcement to suppress workers' voices. One useful approach is to insulate workers from immigration enforcement if the workers help the government enforce workplace laws against employers.

ONE RESPONSE TO this critique of temporary worker statuses is that moving to another country should be a choice for workers to make—even with low wages and poor working conditions.[21] Moreover, temporary workers increase wealth for both sending countries and destination countries when they earn more in other countries than in their own.[22]

But even if temporary workers consent, and even if temporary worker programs increase aggregate global wealth, the concern remains that people in temporary and in-between statuses will become an underclass that's corrosive for a society as a whole. For example, employers could use temporary workers to depress wages and working conditions, and thus to increase their leverage over *all* workers in a destination country. A related concern is that the arrival of newcomers who work may prompt economic anxieties—for example, about financial security and workplace safety—for others already in the job market. I'll explore this issue in a later chapter.[23]

Choices for Migrants

The Swiss writer Max Frisch once reflected, "We asked for workers, but people came."[24] This observation suggests a critique of those who want only labor power but don't want the person who provides it—and think they can get one without the other. Related is the concern that temporary and in-between statuses are permanent in practice. Recall one explanation for these statuses—that they are a stepping-stone toward permission to stay indefinitely. Perhaps they should be assessed as such, so that policymaking is transparent and intentional from the start.

Frisch was right if he meant that no bright line separates workers from people, or the temporary from the indefinite. But his remark doesn't go as far as suggesting that it's best to assess all newcomers as if they will settle indefinitely. Of course, some will stay, but others will leave. Some will never return. Others will go back and forth over a period of years.[25]

Which label—temporary or indefinite—ends up being more accurate shouldn't depend on the irreversible terms of initial admission. Instead, what matters are the choices that both migrants and governments make after arrival. Temporary admissions with a path to citizenship may seem self-contradictory. But this combination responds to the realities of people migrating across national borders and is consistent with respect for the belonging claims of newcomers who become part of communities in the country.

The best approach would allow some migration that is temporary at the start. I've explored the reasons for doing this. But it's vital to recognize that some of these migrants may end up staying for years. An initial decision to let in people temporarily is just the first step. As they become part of communities in the country and thus insiders, respect for their belonging claims requires allowing some to stay indefinitely.

IT'S ALSO ESSENTIAL to integrate newcomers even if their stay isn't cast as indefinite at first. Many will stay indefinitely, and even if they don't, their children and grandchildren may stay. In the United States and a few other countries, future generations will be citizens by birth, and the children of immigrants can become citizens in many other countries. But a path to citizenship is not enough by itself for respecting the belonging claims of newcomers as they become insiders. Integration also is essential to give meaning to citizenship; together they can lead to respect for belonging claims.[26]

This chapter suggests that newcomers, even if granted a temporary or in-between status, should have a viable option to stay once they become part of communities in the country and thus insiders. It's essential to respect their belonging claims by letting them transition to a durable immigration status and ultimately a path to citizenship. As an example of a proposal to do this, the US Senate approved a bill in 2013 that would have let many temporary workers become lawful permanent residents if they had residence and employment for ten years.[27] This would have recognized such transitions as something normal, but the legislation never advanced in the House of Representatives.

A key related aspect of immigration policy with regard to temporary and in-between statuses is giving migrants real options—including returning to a country of origin or engaging in circular migration back and forth. Many migrants leave home reluctantly, and many hope to go back someday. Creating options for return and circular migration is a daunting challenge that I'll analyze in a later chapter. For now, my point is that creating these return and circular migration options is essential for immigration policy, including temporary or in-between statuses, to respect humanity claims and belonging claims.[28]

ONE MORE THOUGHT in this chapter: my analysis may seem to conflict with a core idea that I offered in an earlier book—that it's best to treat newcomers to the United States as Americans in waiting. I explained that this treatment means admitting them as lawful permanent residents and fostering their integration with a presumed path to citizenship.[29]

I still believe it's best to treat all newcomers as future citizens, with an expectation of full belonging. That said, I've just explained why it's a key policy tool to let some newcomers have temporary or in-between statuses. For this tool to be consistent with respect for belonging claims, it's essential to understand that many newcomers will acquire persuasive belonging claims as they gradually become part of communities in the country. It's very hard to know on arrival who will and who won't. In turn, this means that the best way to ensure integration for those who stay is to treat all newcomers as if they might stay indefinitely.

The next question is how to think about another kind of in-between. These are people who live in the country without any formal immigration status—the undocumented. This is the topic of the next chapter, the first of several on immigration outside the law and enforcement.

PART III

Immigration Outside the Law and Enforcement

6

What About People Without Lawful Status?

Over 11 million people live in the United States without lawful immigration status. Many other countries have large numbers of people in similar circumstances.[1] How should these so-called undocumented, unauthorized, or irregular migrants be treated? The answers begin by understanding why so many people in so many countries live without lawful status. By definition, they are violating immigration laws, but the essential deeper inquiry probes the nuances and gravity of this transgression. This chapter explains why legalization is imperative in countries like the United States for borders to respect belonging claims, but that legalization does little lasting good without more fundamental changes going forward.

The history is a good place to start. In an earlier chapter, I examined the history of US immigration and citizenship. I also explained how a civil rights framework emerged to make belonging claims on behalf of noncitizens as well as citizens with aligned interests. Race and religion have been central to that history. It's also a history of labor migration. US immigration policy, reflecting the economy's need for a flexible, cheap workforce, has created and maintained a large unauthorized population. As throughout this book, I'll focus on the United States, but similar themes arise in many countries.[2]

Labor, Race, and Discretion

From the founding of the United States through its westward expansion across the continent, the country relied on newcomers to settle newly acquired territory. They helped to farm it and mine it, and then to work the factories and mills as industrialization spread. Many of these workers came from western and northern Europe. Many were treated with disdain as laborers, or even as people of an inferior "race." Many did dirty, dangerous, and backbreaking work.

Over time, many Europeans—unlike other newcomers—were welcomed as people who would belong. A telling sign was the widespread practice that emerged in the mid-1800s to treat European newcomers like citizens well before they naturalized. They were Americans in waiting who came to enjoy favored positions on the social and economic pyramid.[3]

Other newcomers didn't enjoy the same position or mobility in society. They came to be viewed as suited to agricultural labor or to the lowest rungs of work on the shop floor. Labor and race remained intertwined, as they had been during slavery. In the mid-1800s, the emancipation of slaves and then the conquest and settlement of the West—with forcible displacement of Native peoples—spurred the search for new workers. The US government and employers turned to workers from China and later from elsewhere in Asia. These workers were welcomed at first, especially in the West, to propel the robust economic activity that started with the California Gold Rush in the late 1840s and the building of the transcontinental railroad until 1869.

But economic downturns in the 1870s and 1880s led to a virulent crusade against Asian newcomers, cast as strange invaders. New federal laws severely limited immigration from China, starting in 1882 and continuing until 1943. Other race or nationality restrictions soon took effect to reduce or block immigration from Asia and Africa, at first in federal legislation in 1917, and then in the 1920s with the national origins system designed to prefer immigration from northern and western Europe.[4]

AROUND WHEN FEDERAL laws restricted the arrival of Asian workers in the late 1800s and early 1900s, the demand for Mexican labor grew as technology allowed large-scale agriculture to emerge in the Southwest. Irrigation opened up vast croplands. The refrigerated boxcar made distant markets reachable. Factories in the fields needed armies of workers to plant, tend, harvest, and load crops so they could get to market.

Racial perceptions and federal policymakers cast Mexicans—like Asians before them—as a cheap, subordinate, and disposable workforce. At least as far back as 1848, when the Treaty of Guadalupe-Hidalgo forced Mexico to cede over half of its territory to the United States, people of Mexican ancestry suffered under laws and policies enforcing racial and ethnic segregation and subordination that often resembled Jim Crow for African Americans.

In Mexico, a depressed economy and political turmoil spurred northward migration. This migration may have seemed easier or more natural because of transnational families and other networks on land that had been part of Mexico before it became part of the United States. In contrast to federal immigration law's formal bars to immigration from countries in Asia, geography allowed a different approach toward Mexican workers. Mexico was next door, so employers and the US government could bring in Mexican workers when they were needed. When they weren't needed they could be sent home, or so decision-makers thought.

In 1907, Congress established the Dillingham Commission to "make full inquiry, examination, and investigation . . . into the subject of immigration." In 1911, the Commission's forty-two-volume final report said this about Mexicans:

> Because of their strong attachment to their native land . . . and the possibility of their residence here being discontinued, few become citizens of the United States. The Mexican migrants are providing a fairly adequate supply of labor. . . . While they are not easily assimilated, this is of no very great importance as long as most of them return to their native land. In the case of the Mexican, he is less desirable as a citizen than as a laborer.[5]

Recruitment of Mexican workers with and without lawful status became commonplace as a source of labor for Southwestern agriculture. As more came, they went to other parts of the United States as cheap and flexible labor in a variety of industries, with many employers far from the US–Mexico border.[6]

Mexican workers traveled back and forth across the Mexico–US border in response to employer demand. The US government admitted some as temporary workers. The Bracero program operated from 1942 until the mid-1960s to give employers lawful access to Mexican farmworkers. The government also tolerated substantial migration outside the law—a practical consequence of strong employer demand and minimal resources to patrol spacious borderlands. Workers toiled for low wages in harsh conditions, many without papers.

SELECTIVE ADMISSIONS AND selective enforcement combined with racial perceptions were central to the system. Vast discretion governed arrest, detention, and deportation. At the behest of growers, ranchers, mining companies, railroads, and other employers, the US government restricted migration only selectively. The intensity of enforcement ebbed and flowed. Depending on what economics and politics demanded in any season or year, the government could enforce immigration laws vigorously, or it could tolerate the undocumented.

Congress enacted laws that would enable strict enforcement when needed. In 1929, Congress created the federal crimes of illegal entry and illegal reentry. These laws' supporters saw enforcement through criminal penalties as a way to prevent the dilution of its Anglo-Saxon stock, as a member of Congress put it.[7]

At the same time, agribusiness wanted more cheap labor from Mexico. The way to stop Mexican migrants from settling in the United States, but also to assure a supply of cheap labor, was to rely on discretionary decisions by government officials in collaboration with employers and local governments. Selective enforcement didn't keep undocumented workers from Mexico from doing what many employers considered essential work. But the threat of deportation and criminal charges kept the undocumented scared and in the shadows. The US government did little to prevent or remedy abusive enforcement by federal, state, or local government officials or by private employers and vigilantes. Often, workers in a lawful temporary worker status were marginalized and exploited.

IN 1965, CONGRESS abolished the national origins system and its discriminatory allocation of immigrant admission slots. But other changes in the same decade made it much harder to come lawfully to the United States from Mexico and other countries in Latin America. The 1965 amendments also reworked immigration categories in ways that made it hard for anyone without a college degree to immigrate lawfully based on work. The Bracero program ended formally in 1964 and phased out by 1967, cutting off a major pathway for farmworkers to come temporarily.[8]

A few years later, Congress enacted US immigration law's first annual cap on the total number of new lawful permanent residents from all countries in the Western Hemisphere. Congress also limited the number of lawful permanent residents each year from any single country in all immigration categories combined except immediate relatives. People born in Mexico and a few other countries had to wait longer than people born elsewhere.[9]

But migration networks and patterns, once established, are durable and resist efforts to change them through new laws or enforcement. Sending communities, employers, and workers and their families come to rely on lawful and unlawful migration.[10] With lawful admissions highly restricted but employers eager to hire, it's no wonder that workers kept coming outside the law. The result: a wide gap between the system of lawful admissions in theory and the acquiescence in unauthorized migration in practice.

With over 11 million people without lawful immigration status in the United States now, undocumented workers account for about 5 percent of all workers, and far more in some occupations and industries.[11] Whether someone is arrested, detained, and deported depends on government discretion and bad luck. This pattern, though originally adopted in the context of Mexican migration, has become central to US immigration policy. It seems easy to cast the unauthorized population as lawbreakers, but in fact it's a predictable consequence of an admissions system that's too restrictive to reflect the interests of insiders who want or need more people to come to the United States.[12]

Legalization in Context

Does respect for belonging claims require access to lawful status and a path to citizenship for some undocumented people? Opponents of access to lawful status often deride it as "amnesty." Some supporters of access accept or even embrace the amnesty label. I'll use the term "legalization" because it's literally accurate. Legalization confers legal status.[13]

To answer the question, I'll start by looking at the most recent large-scale legalization program in the United States. A key part of the Immigration Reform and Control Act (IRCA) of 1986 opened a path to lawful status and later to citizenship for several million undocumented residents. At that time, about 3.2 million noncitizens lived in the United States without status. The general legalization program in IRCA allowed about 1.6 million of them become lawful permanent residents. IRCA also included a program that let about 1.1 million undocumented agricultural workers become lawful permanent residents. Many who gained lawful status through these programs later became citizens.[14]

Recent large-scale legalization proposals in the United States have attracted both strong support and strong opposition. A recent example is the US Citizenship Act of 2021, a bill that President Biden sent to Congress on his first day in office.[15] Similar bills have been introduced over several decades, but no legalization program on IRCA's scale has become law since 1986.

IN SMALLER WAYS, US immigration law offers lawful status to people who don't have it. These programs are a type of legalization, even if they aren't labeled as such. In fact, many are taken for granted as basic parts of US immigration law. According to one estimate, from 1986 to 2009 the United States gave lawful immigration status to over 1 million people outside the IRCA general and agricultural legalization programs.[16]

One type of legalization for individuals and families in US law is called cancellation of removal. This term refers to a cluster of statutes, dating back to 1917, that can give lawful status to people who would otherwise be deportable. A current version of one of these statutes allows up to 4,000 noncitizens, almost all of them undocumented, to become lawful permanent residents every year.[17] Applicants must have been physically present in the United States for ten years. They must show that removal would result in exceptional and extremely unusual hardship to a US citizen or permanent resident spouse, minor child, or parent. Criminal convictions can be disqualifying. If applicants meet these requirements, an immigration judge or another government official may exercise discretion to confer lawful permanent residence.

Asylum is seldom considered a form of legalization, but in fact that's one way to understand it. A federal statute sets rules for granting lawful immigration status in the form of asylum to many noncitizens who otherwise would have no lawful status. The asylum system has become so normalized that it's easy to overlook that it offers—for compelling reasons—lawful status to people who arrive without prior permission. It's no accident that asylum skeptics have cast asylum as a way to get around immigration restrictions, using rhetoric against asylum that's often deployed against legalization.

US law offers lawful status in other ways, too. One federal statute authorizes registry, which allows people without status to acquire it if they have been in the United States since 1972. This is now over fifty years ago, but it was fourteen years in the past when the statute set this date in 1986. Another statute authorizes lawful permanent residence for some minors who qualify for Special Immigrant Juvenile Status (SIJS). Other examples are programs that offer lawful status through T and U visas to noncitizens who are victims of crimes or trafficking. Taken together, all of these provisions underscore how small-scale legalization is not unusual.[18]

ONE ACADEMIC STUDY estimated that 30 percent of lawful permanent residents of the United States had been undocumented earlier in their lives. This percentage has fluctuated over time, but it's a basic feature of US immigration policy that some people transition from being undocumented to having a durable status. In the United States, broad-scale legalization has been rare, but legalization on a smaller scale has been ordinary, if contested. In some other countries, broad-scale legalization is more routine. Lawful status for undocumented people is a complex issue, but it's wrong to shut down dialogue by claiming that legalization is rare. What matters is assessing the reasons for and against legalization.[19]

A number of arguments for legalization are rooted in the history that I've recounted in this chapter. People are often undocumented because they want to come to work and employers want to hire them, but lawful status in the United States is very hard to get. As a predictable consequence of US immigration policy, many of the undocumented have long been part of communities in the country. Without lawful status, they are vulnerable to exploitation in the workplace. They and their children have only limited opportunities to integrate into broader society. Treating undocumented people in this way is inconsistent with respect for their belonging claims based on being part of communities in the country—having made homes and playing a substantial social and economic role.[20]

HISTORY SHOWS WHY, as a consequence of official acquiescence, tolerance, or even invitation, no clear moral line separates many people who are undocumented from people with lawful status. Advocates for legalization may wonder why this argument based on the history and structure of US immigration law doesn't persuade more people.

Perhaps it's because the argument rests on a key assumption: that history should shape government decision-making. I understand why some people are wary or opposed to relying on history. That way of approaching immigration policy might seem to suggest treating immigration policy as a site of reparations for past injustices in general. This is a fundamental topic that deserves more attention, which I'll offer in the last chapter of this book.

For now, my point is narrower. Over many decades, US immigration and labor policy has illegalized people. This means that being undocumented shouldn't carry the stigma of a crime or other serious violation. Undocumented people have become parts of communities in the United States. They have belonging claims, many of which may be persuasive. Until immigration policy becomes more consistent with respect for humanity claims and belonging claims, being in the country without lawful status should have a social or cultural meaning that is forgiving and broadly adopted.

Assessing Legalization

The next part of this inquiry is assessing public debate about legalization. The arguments for legalization are generally rooted in the need to respect humanity claims and belonging claims. Each argument suggests legalization for some of the undocumented, but not necessarily for all. The arguments are related to each other and often overlap, but it's helpful to explore them separately.

One argument for legalization emphasizes innocence. This is largely a humanity claim based on the notion that no person should suffer because of the decisions of others in their lives. A core idea is that undocumented young people brought to the United States by their parents or other adults are undocumented through no fault of their own, so nothing justifies denying them lawful status. This perspective is evident in advocacy for the DREAM (Development, Relief, and Education for Alien Minors) Act, which would offer legalization, and for the DACA program. This innocence-based argument has natural appeal, especially when it draws on the compelling stories of accomplished youth.[21]

The flaw in separating "innocent" kids from "guilty" parents in this way is that doing so ignores the history of unauthorized migration. Adults and children aren't undocumented by unconstrained choice. The large unauthorized population reflects selective admissions, selective enforcement, and vast discretion in a system rife with labor exploitation and racial exclusion. Tolerance, acquiescence, and even invitation have produced persistent patterns of unauthorized migration. These policies have hurt both parents and children.[22]

A SECOND ARGUMENT for legalization emphasizes the belonging claims of undocumented people as insiders who are part of communities in the country. Unlike arguments underscoring the innocence of youth, this argument is that legalization is appropriate for all undocumented people with belonging claims. These arguments sometimes refer to earned legalization. This label underscores belonging to a community, perhaps through work, military service, or children.[23]

Time is part of this argument. I explained in the previous chapter why the moment of arrival may not be the best time to decide whether a newcomer should be allowed to stay indefinitely. Similar reasoning applies to legalization. What the undocumented do after arrival should inform any decision to offer lawful status. This timing allows legalization decisions to be better informed and more responsive to the belonging claims of newcomers who become insiders.

A likely objection to this argument's reliance on belonging claims is that the destination country never consented to the undocumented becoming part of communities in the country. But this objection seems to assume incorrectly that the only meaningful consent is explicit. History shows that the United States was quite willing to benefit from undocumented migrants, and that the system reflects a design to make that happen.[24]

A THIRD ARGUMENT overlaps with the second. It's based on the idea that legal rules and society as a whole require finality to move beyond the past. This argument emphasizes that social cohesion suffers if questions linger about status—and thus about the connections among people in the country. This is why a statute of limitations typically sets how long someone has to sue to seek remedy for a wrong, or how long a government has to prosecute someone for a crime. At some point, finality and a fresh start are needed. Until 1952, statutes of limitations applied to immigration violations, but today they are among the few violations with no statute of limitations at all.[25]

Related is the thought that the unauthorized population will remain large for a long time, even with stricter enforcement. Having millions of exploitable undocumented people is corrosive for communities and the country. A large undocumented workforce undercuts wages and working conditions for all workers. Children grow up in the shadows with diminished opportunities that impair them and society as a whole. Out of fear, the undocumented are less likely to cooperate with local law enforcement. They may hesitate to access medical help, with consequences for public health. This is all highly problematic, especially when many undocumented people have become insiders with belonging claims that deserve recognition.[26] From this perspective, legalization helps build a stronger society, just as citizenship helps build a stronger society.[27]

The Rule of Law

Skeptics and opponents of legalization often invoke the "rule of law." They argue that offering lawful status to the undocumented is an incentive for lawbreaking in the future, an unfair preference over people who have been waiting to acquire lawful status through existing pathways, and a reward for lawbreaking in the past. These arguments target legalization both in broad and small-scale programs and on a case-by-case basis. From this perspective, the rule of law demands strict immigration enforcement through arrest, detention, and deportation, or by pushing people to leave.[28]

The argument that legalization incentivizes future lawbreaking is that it will attract more newcomers who hope for similar generosity in the future. Legalization could also influence the behavior of others who might count on the arrival of more people outside the law. Employers might assume a supply of undocumented workers. Traffickers, cartels, and others involved in the migration industry may count on more migrants. Studies show, however, that the prospect of future legalization has little or no effect on the decisions that migrants make to come outside the law. Migration reflects many other, more influential motivations: to work, reunite with relatives, or escape dire conditions.[29]

What about the objection that legalization unfairly prefers the undocumented over people using existing pathways and often waiting in a long line? One response is to make sure that people waiting for their immigration slots gain admission at the same time as anyone benefitting from legalization. This mechanism was part of federal legislation that passed the US Senate in 2013 but never got anywhere in the House.[30] Beyond this, the deeper question is whether it's unfair to have legalization when others have been standing in line. The answer depends on how to view legalization most accurately. For anyone not persuaded by the reasons for legalization, then offering any sort of lawful status to the undocumented is likely to prompt objections. But persuasive reasons for legalization can override concerns that it grants unfair preferences for the undocumented.

THE MOST BASIC rule of law argument insists that legalization is wrong because it rewards lawbreaking. But it's unconvincing to cite the rule of law mechanically and stop there without delving deeper. History is littered with laws imposing requirements that later generations disavowed. Slavery is a notorious example, but there's no shortage of others. These examples show that legal rules can undermine the rule of law if those rules are applied mechanically.[31]

As I've explained in this chapter, unlawful presence in the United States is inconclusive by design. The system has created a large unauthorized population. Government choices—discretionary and often discriminatory—decide who is snared in the enforcement net. Legalization shrinks the universe of decisions in which discretionary enforcement choices run the risk of improper decision-making. From a rule of law perspective, this is an important virtue.

US immigration law shows some awareness of this problem. Key is the willingness to make exceptions to strict application of the letter of the law. Examples include some in-between statuses like parole, Temporary Protected Status (TPS), and Deferred Action for Childhood Arrivals (DACA).

Similar receptivity is evident in laws that don't confer lawful status but otherwise recognize the undocumented as part of communities. Many employment laws try to protect undocumented workers from safety and health violations, employment discrimination, and substandard pay. The undocumented are guaranteed elementary and secondary education and are eligible for some public benefits. Federal, state, and local tax schemes apply to all people regardless of immigration status.[32]

Some people may view these measures as protections for workers other than undocumented workers. The thought is that protecting the undocumented will reduce incentives for employers to hire the undocumented to depress the wages and working conditions of other workers. But in fact, any such effect confirms a basic truth: that undocumented workers are part of workplace communities. If they were separate workforces, the treatment of undocumented workers wouldn't have this effect on the treatment of other workers.

All of these laws and policies to avoid strict application of immigration law are small legalizations, issue by issue and case by case. Broader measures would consolidate these small legalizations, but the basic rationale would be the same—to offset an immigration policy that led to millions of people coming and staying without status. This is why legalization is a principled policy tool that advances the rule of law.

The Limits of Legalization

Designing any legalization program requires answering lots of questions. Who is eligible, and does eligibility include family members? Will it be limited to only some undocumented people? Will the undocumented get lawful permanent resident status immediately, or an interim status first? Will they have a path to citizenship? What fees must applicants or their sponsors pay? Who will decide about applications, how, and how long will a decision take? Will people using existing pathways also get lawful status, to address concerns that legalization lets the undocumented cut the line?

Some of the answers will depend on the rationales behind any legalization program. For example, some might argue that undocumented children are more innocent than the adults who brought them to the United States. This reasoning suggests legalization for childhood arrivals, but not for all undocumented people. Or if the idea is to recognize that the undocumented become parts of communities in the country, eligibility criteria could reflect this purpose. For example, the general legalization program in IRCA required a certain period of residence and some English-language competence. Legalization programs might require that applicants have been employed, in school, or in the military. Or they could offer status only to undocumented workers in certain occupations or industries, perhaps only "essential workers"—a term often applied to agricultural workers and medical personnel.[33]

I've assumed so far that a legalization program would be a broadscale program like the general program in IRCA. An alternative is to expand case-by-case legalization through cancellation of removal and other discretionary mechanisms. A more generous standard for hardship might apply, and government officials could consider hardship to a broader group of people, including to the noncitizens themselves. This sort of case-by-case approach would, like broad-scale legalization, require legislative changes to eligibility criteria and approval standards. It would also require an increase in funding support for deciding cases, and it would run some risk of decisions that are inconsistent, arbitrary, standardless, or biased.

BEYOND THESE DESIGN questions, proponents of legalization need to recognize its inherent limitations. By offering lawful status, legalization initially decreases the number of undocumented people. But one-time legalization—even a large-scale program—can only do so much. Without other changes, the remaining undocumented population will start immediately to grow again. Given this limit on what legalization can do, its champions need to be wary of paying too high a political and societal price—perhaps some combination of restrictions on asylum, draconian border enforcement, massive enforcement budgets, and expanded detention in private prisons.

For legalization to matter in the medium and long term, it might need to repeat on some sort of cycle. Otherwise, legalization will help noncitizens in the country by the cutoff date, but it will help no one who arrives afterward. One option for letting legalization repeat on a cycle is a rule that allows anyone who has lived in the country for a certain period of time—regardless of immigration status—to become a lawful permanent resident. Earlier in this chapter I noted that US law already has one provision that could operate this way.

Called registry, it allows lawful permanent residence for almost anyone with continuous residence since a date specified in the statute. The first version became law in 1929. It offered lawful permanent residence to people who had entered the United States by June 3, 1921. Congress has updated the statute several times, most recently in 1986 to require entry before January 1, 1972—over fourteen years earlier. This 1972 cutoff date remains, so the required period now exceeds fifty years, and registry's practical effect has virtually disappeared. In FY 2021, only forty-eight of 740,002 new lawful permanent residents relied on registry.[34]

For registry to be effective as a form of periodic legalization, the cutoff date would need to be updated regularly to something closer to the present than the fourteen-year mark in the 1986 legislation. An alternative is to avoid a fixed cut-off date, and instead to specify a period of time. With either approach, the result would be a rolling legalization rather than one available only at a snapshot moment. A much less reliable alternative is a political culture that enacts periodic legalizations as a core feature of immigration policy.

ROLLING OR PERIODIC legalizations, registry, or a statute of limitations would be better than legalization once every forty or fifty years, but these sorts of measures are Band-Aids. The long-term solution is fixing core features of the immigration system to minimize the number of noncitizens without lawful status. It's misguided procrastination to adopt legalizations without reforming the system as a whole.

Instead of offering lawful status to the undocumented, what about the alternative of ramping up enforcement? Several questions follow. Can immigration enforcement respect the humanity claims of all people? Can enforcement respect the belonging claims of insiders? I'll answer these questions in the next chapter when I look at the flipside of legalization.

7

What Should Enforcement Do, and Not Do?

B asic to any country's immigration system are rules to grant or deny permission for noncitizens to enter or remain. In this chapter, I'll assess how governments and their officials and employees put these rules into practical effect through enforcement. The idea that national borders must respect the humanity claims of all and belonging claims of insiders explains why some enforcement practices are deeply troubling.[1]

Borders don't always require enforcement. They could be open. All over the world, many physical national borders go virtually unenforced, or are porous for some or most people. Borders between states of the United States are unenforced, except for agricultural inspection between some states. That said, I focus in this chapter on the many national borders that come with enforcement efforts. This is true not just for the physical border, but also for national borders in a broader sense— whenever it matters whether someone is a citizen or not.

I'LL START WITH the recent history of immigration enforcement in the United States. Some enforcement tries to deter or prevent immigration violations. Governments issue documents, monitor entry, and conduct surveillance. These activities directly affect noncitizens outside the physical border. Enforcement also takes place—often more visibly—at or inside the physical border, by applying rules that authorize the arrest, detention, and deportation of some noncitizens.

It also matters who participates in immigration enforcement by making the rules, setting policy, or doing the enforcing in practice. The US Congress enacts statutes that address various aspects of federal enforcement. Congress also provides money for enforcement. Within the statutory framework, the federal executive branch adopts enforcement regulations, rules, policies, and practices.[2]

Inside the executive branch, the president and White House staff get involved, especially when immigration is central in national politics. In addition, the Department of Homeland Security has a leading role, but other departments, especially the Departments of Justice, Labor, Health and Human Services, and State, make key decisions. Within each agency, decision-makers include a range of personnel from top officials in Washington, DC, to low-level officers and employees in scattered field offices. Federal courts preside over lawsuits that decide if enforcement decisions are lawful.

State and local governments also can be involved. The federal government might delegate enforcement authority that states and localities may agree to exercise. Or they might decide on their own to bolster federal enforcement, sometimes against federal wishes and sometimes with federal approval. Other states and localities do the opposite, for example by adopting laws and policies to limit cooperation with federal immigration agencies.

Immigration enforcement also has a large private component that includes employers, transport companies, schools and universities, and other private and public actors. For example, federal law requires most employers to check employees for identity documents and work permits. Most immigration detention takes place at private facilities, and data collection and management are largely in private hands.[3]

Intensifying Immigration Enforcement

Assessing enforcement starts with overall familiarity with the trend to intensify immigration enforcement in recent decades, and in many countries. This overview mentions only major developments in the United

States since the 1990s, but similar patterns have appeared in many countries that have seen the arrival of migrants in great numbers since the turn of the twenty-first century.

In the United States, immigration violations—especially unlawful crossings of the US–Mexico border—intensified as hot-button political issues in the 1990s. The federal government ramped up immigration enforcement, and in key states, immigration enforcement became a priority for some elected officials. The passage of Proposition 187 in California in 1994 was a sign of this trend.[4] This ballot initiative tried to deny undocumented children a public elementary and secondary education, and made the undocumented ineligible for public benefits. Its overall purpose was to express intolerance of federal immigration law violations and to make life harder for the undocumented so that they would leave California.

Federal courts kept almost all of Proposition 187 from taking effect. They reasoned that it improperly conflicted with the US Constitution on access to education and with federal laws on public benefits. But the real effects of Proposition 187 would take time to emerge. It marked a shift in state, local, and federal politics. Influential voices called for more immigration enforcement. In the mid-1990s, the administration of Democratic President Bill Clinton focused US–Mexico border enforcement on preventing unauthorized crossings rather than apprehending many but not all people after they had crossed.[5]

In 1996, new federal legislation intensified enforcement, with bipartisan support in Congress and President Clinton's signature. The new law expanded the categories of noncitizens who could be excluded or deported. For example, a broader range of criminal convictions could lead to deportation. The legislation also imposed new penalties for unlawful presence in the United States. It limited eligibility for the case-by-case exceptions that had let some noncitizens avoid the immigration consequences of crimes. In addition, the 1996 legislation expanded and sometimes required the detention of noncitizens as their cases were being decided. Relatedly, Congress swelled the enforcement budget, for example with appropriations for massive new hiring by the US Border Patrol and other agencies.[6]

Many states and localities amplified these federal efforts with their own measures and resources. Some state and local governments tried to keep the undocumented from finding work or housing. Others adopted measures to check more aggressively that all employees in the state had federal permission to work. Some states and localities limited access to public higher education or to other benefits such as financial support and health care.[7]

Going in the opposite direction, some states and localities tried to curtail federal immigration enforcement through what are often called sanctuary laws and policies. These efforts typically tried to limit state and local cooperation with federal immigration agencies. State and local governments also adopted measures to integrate noncitizens regardless of immigration status. For instance, they issued driver's licenses and identification documents, allowed access to higher education on the same basis as US citizens, and opened up state-funded medical care and other public benefits regardless of immigration status.[8]

Enforcement and Discretion

Humanity claims to challenge enforcement are persuasive when it is too severe—when enforcement puts migrants at risk of drowning at sea or dying of thirst, separates children from parents, or imprisons people in inhumane conditions or for prolonged periods. Humanity claims can also be persuasive when the decision-making process is unfair—as when the government won't hear noncitizens' arguments why they should be let in or allowed to stay.

What about belonging claims? A core belonging claim asks for treatment that respects that someone is an insider. To illustrate, suppose a high percentage of immigration arrests in a city occur in neighborhoods where most residents trace their ancestry to Mexico or a country in Central America. The police make markedly fewer arrests in neighborhoods with many residents of Irish ancestry. This pattern amounts to unequal treatment of the first neighborhood. Some of its residents may be undocumented, and some may be citizens, lawful permanent residents, or other noncitizens in lawful status. All of these people could be insiders who will suffer if immigration agents disproportionately arrest them, their relatives, their friends, or their neighbors.

This scenario prompts a likely counterargument: What's wrong with enforcing immigration law against violators? In answering this question, my focus is not on the letter of the laws that are enforced, but rather on *how* they are enforced. When does enforcement itself disrespect the belonging claims of insiders? Imagine a stretch of road in a mountainous area with enough curves and blind spots that a speed limit is necessary to minimize accidents. But also imagine that the posted speed limit is much lower than usual for the region—even for mountain roads— and that almost everyone drives faster than the limit. Police issue lots of speeding tickets, but police budgets are meager. Voluntary compliance is incomplete, and police can't stop every violator.

This approach to speed limits resembles immigration enforcement in the United States and many countries. When resources available for enforcement aren't enough to achieve a level of high compliance, government officials and employees must make some decisions. Some are broad-scale choices about resources. Will funding be increased? Will funding be increased but still be inadequate? In traffic enforcement, will new funds go to officers, road signs, radar guns, or vehicles? In immigration enforcement, will new funds go to personnel, border walls, ports of entry, workplace raids, computer databases, or prisons for immigration detention?

Other enforcement decisions reflect discretionary choices on a smaller scale. Will traffic enforcement focus on any particular stretch of road? At what hours or on which days of the week? Will immigration enforcement target some neighborhoods more than others? Will immigration enforcement target some types of violations over others? Should noncitizens with criminal convictions be a high priority for arrest, detention, and deportation? Should undocumented people brought to the country as children be a low priority?

Why this broad array of consequential choices? The answer is the gap between what the law says and what actually happens. If resources and political commitment to enforcement were sufficient to eliminate the gap between law on the books and law in action, then discretion wouldn't matter much. But the large gap in immigration law means that government officials and employees have vast discretion to enforce selectively.[9]

In immigration law, this large gap also gives the federal government the option to delegate some enforcement authority—and thus some discretionary decisions—to other people and institutions. These may be states or localities that arrest and transfer noncitizens to federal immigration officials, private employers who check for federal work permission, or private prison companies that hold noncitizens in detention.

Discretion and Discrimination

It's time to look closely at the vast discretion at the core of immigration enforcement. Discretion can be a good thing. Discretionary decisions devote resources where they are needed. Discretion can also fit outcomes to the circumstances of each case. This is valuable flexibility when many of the relevant legal rules are set out in general terms that don't foresee the variations in facts that arise.

But enforcement discretion is fraught. It can conceal decisions that disrespect humanity claims or belonging claims. For example, government officials might choose to let some migrants drift on rickety boats in treacherous seas or die of thirst in burning deserts. Or discretion might mean applying entry restrictions more harshly to people from majority-Muslim countries than to people from majority-Christian countries. Discretion can lead to discrimination in arrest patterns inside national borders. Even if it's possible to count arrests, detentions, and deportations, it's hard to tell if enforcement decisions reflect racial discrimination or inaccuracies in the process for identifying immigration law violators.[10]

TRANSPARENCY IS INDISPENSABLE for minimizing these problems with discretionary decisions. Detection and remedy are essential, but equally important are systems to prevent harms. One way to enhance transparency and accountability in immigration enforcement through both prevention and remedy is to publicize prosecutorial discretion guidelines that set out enforcement priorities. The goal is to identify some categories of potentially deportable noncitizens as high enforcement priorities and other categories as low priorities. Publicizing priorities can prompt healthy debate. People might push back if they believe it's wrong to use criminal convictions to prioritize the deportation of some long-time residents. Others might argue for stepping up enforcement against noncitizens in low priority categories.

The US government has published such guidelines for decades, but officials and employees in the field have sometimes been reluctant to publicize them. The attitude may be that the government should never publicly identify any deportable noncitizen as a low enforcement priority, because doing so undermines the deterrence that effective enforcement requires. In other words, compliance is greater if violators don't know what the government will do. But this view risks improper enforcement, especially rogue decisions that conflict with internal priorities. Limiting this risk requires enforcement priorities, public guidelines, and systems to put those priorities into practice.[11]

This is one major virtue of the Deferred Action for Childhood Arrivals (DACA) program in the United States. It took discretionary enforcement decisions away from field officers in Immigration and Customs Enforcement (ICE)—the enforcement branch of the Department of Homeland Security (DHS)—shifting them to a unit trained for this purpose in US Citizenship and Immigration Services (USCIS), the part of DHS that decides immigration benefits. This shift centralized and systematized the exercise of discretion, and so enhanced transparency and accountability.[12]

These ways to enhance transparency and accountability contrast sharply with a Trump administration order that deviated from all other modern presidential administrations by declaring all immigration violators to be priorities for enforcement. The order claimed to eliminate discretion in immigration enforcement, but in fact, that was not its practical effect. As long as resources, political will, and the economy's need for workers don't allow complete enforcement, someone will be making discretionary decisions about enforcement. The Trump order's practical effect was to delegate discretion to low-level officials, burying enforcement decisions out of sight.[13]

Approaches to Immigration Enforcement

One way to address the problem of opaque discretionary decisions is to close the gap between what the law says and what actually happens. In an earlier chapter, I explored legalization as a way to do this. Some might respond by suggesting a different strategy: to intensify enforcement even more, starting with further significant increases in enforcement resources.[14]

Blocking this approach are the forces that have led to a large unauthorized population in many countries—in the United States, about 11 million people. The US immigration system tolerates, acquiesces in, and even invites people to live and work without status. Demand for workers is strong, but a selective admissions system lets only a limited number of newcomers come and stay lawfully. The type of enforcement that might transform immigration patterns would run into strong resistance from the many insiders who benefit from today's system.

The conditions that would allow immigration enforcement to respect humanity claims and belonging claims would require a system that's fully restructured along the lines that I explain throughout this book. But working toward that goal requires smaller steps. This approach underscores the need to assume that enforcement will continue in some form, making it essential to evaluate current general approaches to enforcement.

Walls

The high wall on the US–Mexico border shunts border crossers to desert terrain with a high risk of death from thirst and heat exhaustion. Migrants trying to scale the wall have fallen and suffered serious injuries including paralysis. These predictable consequences of this wall are so extreme that they reflect disrespect for the humanity claims of all, even those with no connection to the United States.[15]

To be sure, it's possible to make borders so impervious that they wouldn't allow any crossings at all. This sort of wall would avoid the risks that I've mentioned. But then this barrier would run a risk of blocking access to the protection that forced migrants seek when they reach the border, and thus would be troubling as disrespect for their humanity claims.

Another fundamental problem is that walls disrespect humanity claims when they keep out some people based on their race or religion. Does building a high border wall reflect improper discrimination? Proponents of walls may argue that they are needed to stave off illegal crossings. And it's intuitive that barriers erected on national borders will dissuade some crossings, even if making border crossing more difficult can add to the unauthorized population of the United States by discouraging travel back and forth.[16]

More pertinent to discrimination is that the Trump administration's plan to fortify and build out a wall on the US–Mexico border was a symbol of animosity toward the Mexican migrants—a group that Trump vilified as a candidate and as president. But a substantial percentage of undocumented people in the United States didn't cross from Mexico without inspection. They came from many countries and overstayed their terms of admission. Devoting enforcement resources to target one group of noncitizens disrespects both the humanity claims of all noncitizens and the belonging claims of insiders who are closely connected to those noncitizens.[17]

Detention

The term "immigration detention" refers to locking up noncitizens who violate immigration laws. But detention is a euphemism for imprisonment, as is clear to anyone who has seen the outside and inside of these facilities. One rationale for detention is to make sure that noncitizens appear for immigration hearings. This reason has some appeal, but studies suggest that providing noncitizens with lawyers would be at least as effective in limiting no-shows. Another reason for detention is to deter immigration law violations, especially unlawful border crossings. Even if this is true, immigration detention, like any prison, is inherently severe, so the reasons to detain call for serious assessment.[18]

Immigration detention allows the government and private contractors to inflict pain and trauma on some violators. This alone can be enough to disrespect the humanity claims of any detainee, and the belonging claims of any detained noncitizens who are insiders, especially when detention is prolonged and might even last years. Detention may also disrespect the belonging claims of insiders who are closely connected to anyone who is detained. Only some noncitizens in immigration detention are allowed to seek release by posting bond, and that option is often financially out of reach.

Another problem is that detaining noncitizens undermines the accuracy of decisions in their cases. In the United States, it's very hard to get a volunteer lawyer's help in the remote locations of most detention facilities. Without lawyers, detained noncitizens find it especially hard to make their arguments for favorable outcomes under federal law. Many give up on their cases by disengaging with the process or accepting deportation. These risks associated with unfair process undermine respect for humanity claims and belonging claims.[19]

Inadequate Process

I've just observed that immigration detention can undermine the accuracy of decisions. Lack of due process is a problem throughout immigration systems. Respect for humanity claims and belonging claims requires fair rules applied through fair process. But noncitizens often find it impossible to counter allegations that they have violated immigration laws and that they have no relief from deportation. In the United States, nothing requires the federal government to provide noncitizens—not even children—with a lawyer at no expense, so legal assistance requires some savvy plus financial means or finding a volunteer to provide legal counsel.[20]

These challenges are heightened when—as often is true—immigration judges decide cases on quick timelines, notice of hearings and deadlines is inadequate, language barriers impede communication, long delays hinder the process, or judges don't explain their decisions. Without due process in enforcement, the borders being enforced will disrespect humanity claims and belonging claims.[21]

Criminal Penalties

Criminal penalties may seem more focused on serious wrongdoing than walls and detention are, but disrespect for humanity claims and belonging claims are still a serious problem if criminal penalties are excessively harsh or reflect improper discrimination. Whether either is true requires asking more questions. Should some immigration violations be crimes? And why are some violations penalized as crimes, but others aren't? In many countries, unauthorized migration is not a crime. In the United States, federal law says that unlawful entry and reentry are crimes, but it's not a crime to overstay or violate other terms of admission. Is crossing the border without permission a more serious form of wrongdoing?

Establishing crimes based on immigration violations also may disrespect humanity claims or belonging claims if the penalty is too harsh. The same history of immigration policy that matters in assessing legalization matters here, too. If unlawful presence is a natural consequence of decisions to tolerate, acquiesce in, or even invite unauthorized migration, criminal penalties may be disproportionate.

Another troubling aspect of criminal penalties arises when the government can decide to use the threat of criminal prosecution to pressure migrants to give up on lawful options to stay. For example, the government might agree not to punish unlawful entry with anything stiffer than time already spent in jail, but only on the condition that the border crosser gives up any claims that might lead to permission to stay. This sort of coercion disrespects humanity claims to the fair application of immigration restrictions.[22]

Criminalizing an immigration violation may also disrespect humanity claims and belonging claims when the criminal penalty or its application reflects discrimination. Illegal entry and illegal reentry are federal crimes based on a statute enacted in 1929. Its purpose was to intensify enforcement against Mexican migrants, whom congressional leaders saw as a threat to the racial purity of the predominantly Anglo-Saxon majority of the US population.[23]

The racist origins of a statute that makes a violation into a crime don't prove that it's racist to file criminal charges based on the statute today. The relationship between past and present racism poses complex questions that I'll explore in this book's last chapter. Here my point is narrower—that prosecuting immigration violations as crimes is a potential site of discrimination. It's essential to examine criminal penalties to see if they reflect discrimination today or the persistence of past discrimination, and if they thus disrespect the humanity claims of all people and the belonging claims of insiders.

Privatized Enforcement

In the United States, most of the prison beds available on any given night for potential deportees are provided by private for-profit companies under contracts with the federal government. Delegating this aspect of government enforcement to private companies is problematic. A profit motive can skew decisions—as to both operations and lobbying strategies—toward making money instead of complying with standards required by law or contract. And discretionary immigration enforcement decisions by private companies may be especially difficult to monitor.[24]

Similar troubling aspects of delegating power arise whenever governments deputize private enforcers. In the United States, federal law requires most employers to check that employees have work permission under federal immigration law. Employers can use this power to check more closely or more often the documents of workers who complain about wages and working conditions or who make trouble in other ways. Other private parties have an official role in immigration enforcement. They include airlines and other common carriers, which typically must enforce documentation requirements for travelers.[25]

When an even broader group of private parties—including vigilantes—decide to apprehend people that they suspect of immigration violations, enforcement can become even more opaque, with increased risk of discrimination or lack of fair process. In all of these areas of privatized enforcement, the problem is a lack of transparency that undermines accountability, and which in turn creates a significant risk of disrespect for both humanity claims and belonging claims.[26]

State and Local Enforcement

Related concerns about opaque immigration enforcement decisions arise in the United States when states and localities participate in enforcement. This might happen when the federal government delegates authority to states or localities, or when they decide on their own to bolster federal enforcement. In these settings or in other countries where similar conditions prevail, state and local enforcement activity may disrespect humanity claims or belonging claims.

Consider Arizona's Senate Bill 1070, which the state legislature enacted in 2010 to expand the state and local role in immigration enforcement. The Obama administration argued—and the US Supreme Court agreed—that the Arizona law was invalid because it was inconsistent with federal laws on immigration, and therefore was preempted. But at stake was more than federal versus state turf.[27]

The legal doctrine at the heart of the Supreme Court's decision was federal preemption of state laws, but the more fundamental concern was that state and local officials and employees would discriminate in enforcement. Much of the federal government's argument was based on concerns about the effects of SB 1070 on Latinx communities. It was no coincidence that the federal government brought this challenge at the same time it was investigating Sheriff Joe Arpaio of Maricopa County—the largest county in Arizona and one of the largest counties in the country. The federal investigation probed his department's practice of targeting Latinx communities for immigration raids.

In this setting, a compelling reason to restrict state and local enforcement was to limit the risk that state and local police would disrespect the belonging claims of insiders who would suffer from discriminatory enforcement of federal immigration law. This connection became more clear when other lawsuits, by individuals and organizations, tried to block SB 1070 and similar laws in other states. These lawsuits generally alleged a combination of preemption and unlawful discrimination.[28]

Databases

From the perspective of humanity claims and belonging claims, much of the problem with vast enforcement discretion is a lack of transparency and accountability. What's unknown can't be checked, and what's not checked can't be prevented or fixed. It's possible that solutions can emerge if enforcement decisions can be restructured to minimize discretion. One way to reduce discretion is to close the gap between the law on the books and the law in action. But if that gap remains wide, it might reduce discretion to rely more on enforcement techniques that use automated systems—for example, to check for permission to work. But the use of automated systems can itself involve an exercise of discretion in enforcement that calls for transparency and accountability.[29]

For instance, state and local police in the United States routinely want to check if anyone they arrest is wanted for other offenses. To do this, they check the arrestee's identity against a federal database. This check might reveal to the federal government that the arrestee is a noncitizen who may be deportable. It's tempting to think that routinely checking the immigration status of all arrestees takes discretion out of the process. But it doesn't. The initial decision to arrest can reflect stereotypes and biases about who should be caught and punished. This might be the sort of racial or religious discrimination that disrespects humanity claims or belonging claims. From this perspective, arrest patterns may be a problem that automatic reliance on databases won't solve.[30]

Enforcement Outside Physical Borders

Enforcement may disrespect humanity claims and belonging claims if it relies on government decisions outside a country's physical border, especially if that location lets them avoid oversight. Several features of US law have this effect. The plenary power doctrine insulates the federal government's immigration decisions from challenges based on the US Constitution. This insulation is greater for decisions that affect noncitizens who are outside the country.[31]

In addition, many US laws that constrain the government's immigration decisions don't apply outside the country. For example, a federal statute obligates the US government to accept asylum applications, but only if the applicant reaches the physical border. This rule is the legal basis for enforcement that interdicts asylum seekers on the high seas to keep them from accessing the protection system.[32]

Enforcement Reform and Its Limits

I've explained in this chapter how many current approaches to enforcement may disrespect the humanity claims of all people or the belonging claims of insiders. My purpose here isn't to argue categorically to modify or abolish particular approaches to enforcement, but instead to provide a conceptual and analytical framework for evaluation. This framework suggests that some widely adopted practices are more troubling than they might first appear. Some problems can be fixed, but other practices are more concerning—perhaps for reasons that may not be apparent at first.

Is there any enforcement that doesn't disrespect humanity claims or belonging claims? My answer starts with the idea of realistic utopia that I explain in the Introduction. The realistic facet prompts me to explore what it would take to make enforcement more likely to respect humanity claims and belonging claims. It turns out that realistic reforms are quite possible in each of the areas that I've examined in this chapter.

One reform is legal representation to ensure fair hearings for all noncitizens facing immigration enforcement. Another is restricting reliance on detention and improving conditions in detention that remains. It's also crucial to rethink who has enforcement authority and to insist on more transparency and accountability in enforcement decisions.

These reforms require systems that can accomplish key tasks. One is to identify, investigate, and discipline violations. Another is to hold government personnel and private actors liable to compensate people when enforcement against them inflicts bodily harm. A third is to require the federal government to bring back noncitizens that it wrongly deported. This isn't an exhaustive list, but it should convey a sense of what sorts of reforms deserve serious consideration and can make a difference.[33]

BEYOND THESE REFORMS, the only ways to make enforcement more likely to respect humanity claims and belonging claims is more fundamental—to close the large gap between what the law says and what actually happens. Though it's possible to read this as a plea for more enforcement, that reading suggests steps that would be misguided because they would enforce and reinforce aspects of national borders that already disrespect humanity claims and belonging claims.

In previous chapters, I suggested better solutions. These include changing rules for letting people in and offering lawful status for many noncitizens without it. In later chapters, I'll explore other approaches. Unless the system is changed in fundamental ways, enforcement will only amplify an immigration system's flaws—a response as futile as reacting to drug addiction with more police and prisons.[34]

PART IV

Delving Deeper

8

How Can We Take Skeptics
Seriously, and Why?

Many people in destination countries are skeptical or hostile toward immigration. They voice their concerns and anxieties in different ways, often saying that newcomers make things worse for people already in the country. A core question is how to address these concerns and anxieties consistent with respect for humanity claims and belonging claims. I'll explain in this chapter why it's essential to address economic anxieties generated by immigration, and why failure to do so undermines potential support for better responses to immigration and allows demagogues to mobilize cultural and racial anxiety.

In earlier chapters, I focused on immigrants who are insiders because they are part of communities in a country, but whose belonging claims are neglected.[1] It's also essential to pay attention to another group of insiders that decision-makers may neglect—insiders that may see the effects of immigration as harmful. Some of these skeptics or opponents may be citizens. Some may have been in the country for generations. Some may belong to groups, such as African Americans in the United States, who already suffer under historically rooted disadvantage. The arrival of newcomers can prompt concern among all of these groups, either about the number of newcomers or about being shut out of the process for deciding immigration policy.

How might the treatment of insiders who are concerned about the possible negative effects of immigration be a way of respecting these insiders' belonging claims? First, it's crucial to recognize that economic anxieties are just part of the perception that immigrants cause harm in destination countries. Talking about economics often reflects deeper anxieties, resentments, and prejudices. The arrival of newcomers might alter the population by race, ethnicity, religion, language, or in other ways. These deeper concerns, not economics, may be the real issue.[2]

But addressing deeper concerns requires first taking economic effects and perceptions seriously. No conscientious policymaker can brush aside economic grievances. Dismissive responses invite festering falsehoods and the self-pity of victimhood. The result is fertile ground for resentment, animosity, and hate. Opposition to immigration will get more traction if little is done to address the economic effects of immigration and how those effects are perceived.

Immigration's Economic Effects

Advocates for more robust immigration often point to the consensus among economists that immigration boosts the national economy as a whole. New workers produce more, and new consumers buy more. These gains multiply as newcomers integrate over generations into the economy and society in general.[3]

But these statements about the economy as a whole don't engage with what matters politically and culturally. We need to ask: Exactly how does immigration affect the economy? Who wins and who loses? Over what period of time? These concerns about winners and losers are at the heart of immigration politics. The truth is nuanced, but it's crucial to take seriously the view that immigrants have some adverse economic effects on some insiders. The basic idea is that immigrants compete for jobs, so whenever they find work, they may diminish or limit wages and working conditions for people already in the workforce.[4]

The need to respect the belonging claims of insiders is relevant to economic anxiety in two ways. First, if immigration benefits some insiders but hurts other insiders, then the outcome is to prefer some insiders over others. This is inconsistent with respect for belonging claims. Second, a widespread belief that immigration hurts insiders economically can generate backlash against immigrants. This backlash can undermine the integration that's indispensable as newcomers become insiders.[5]

ECONOMISTS HAVE ANALYZED migration's impact on domestic labor markets. In the United States, a pioneering study in 1990 by Nobel Prize-winning economist David Card evaluated the impact of about 45,000 Cubans who arrived in Miami in 1980. The analysis is now several decades old, but its approach and the debate that it generated still illustrate both the consensus and the dimensions of disagreement in many countries.[6]

The newcomers in Card's research were some of the 125,000 people who traveled on boats to the United States from the port of Mariel during a temporary loosening of Cuban exit controls. Card assessed how these migrants' entry into the job market affected US workers. He compared unemployment in Miami with unemployment in four similar US cities: Tampa, Atlanta, Houston, and Los Angeles.[7] Card found no adverse effects on employment or wages for US workers (including African Americans), who did better in Miami than in the four other cities. He showed that though these Cuban migrants entered the workforce, they also generated new demand for goods and services. Businesses grew. More people in the same job market didn't mean more unemployment.[8]

What explains Card's findings? The key fact is that many newcomers don't displace the current workforce by doing the same work. Instead, they are complementary workers who do different jobs.[9] This means that new workers can create jobs indirectly by putting employers on a firmer footing. In addition, many newcomers become entrepreneurs who hire people.

MORE FUNDAMENTALLY, REDUCING immigration won't be enough
to improve wages and working conditions inside the country. Wage
stagnation and unemployment have many causes that include international trade; technology and automation; outsourcing; market con-
centration that reduces worker bargaining power; a static minimum
wage; the decline of unions; the privatization of government; insufficient funding for public education; and the growth of temporary,
part-time, or gig-based work. Immigration is just one factor, certainly
not the most important one, and perhaps not much of a factor at all.
It's wrong to put the blame on immigration when the combination of
these other factors has created the real problem for workers already in
the country—a free market shaped by the liberalization of international
trade.[10]

Findings by Card and others regarding the effects of newcomers on
labor markets in various countries have won broad acceptance among
economists, but they have not convinced everyone. The economist
George Borjas has published research that generally reaches different
results; he concludes that many low-wage US workers compete for work
with immigrants, and that these workers are worse off economically than
they would be without immigrant competition.[11]

The consensus among economists seems to be that immigration is
good for the economy as a whole and in the long run. But what matters
politically isn't whether Card or Borjas should be declared the winner of
the debate between them. The apparent lessons from any study by them
or others depend on focus, assumptions, and time horizon—whether
it examines broad groups and long-term gains or smaller groups in the
short term. Central to the making of immigration policy that respects
the belonging claims of insiders is how newcomers affect—and are perceived to affect—smaller but significant groups of people in workplaces
and communities.

A key fact for political impact is the perception that policymakers don't care. Closely related is the perception that a select group of
insiders—many of them the affluent in urban and suburban areas—take
the overall gains from immigration and leave little if anything for others.

I'll say more about this political impact after I examine fiscal impact and the view that immigrants are a drain on federal, state, and local treasuries.[12]

Immigration's Effects on Public Treasuries

Along with the view that immigrants take jobs from existing workers, some skeptics or opponents of immigration express concern that taxes paid by immigrants don't cover public funding for education, healthcare, and other services. But effects on public treasuries are nuanced. Many levels of government collect revenues from people regardless of their immigration status. In the United States, the same tax laws apply inside the country to all people. This is true for income taxes and sales taxes, and for property taxes paid directly or in rent. Many workers—including the undocumented—contribute to Social Security.[13]

In assessing revenues and expenditures, questions about immigration and public treasuries don't produce clear answers. As with labor market effects, any study's findings will reflect its assumptions and the time period it examines. Many immigrants are high earners who pay substantial taxes. Other newcomers earn less and pay less in taxes, reflecting low levels of training and experience or limited job market access. But this is just a snapshot of current payments. It's hard to say what their children and grandchildren will do. And yet looking into the future must be part of a full assessment of fiscal impact.[14]

Another wrinkle: the governments that collect taxes and other revenues aren't always the ones that fund the services that newcomers use. In the United States, many undocumented workers pay federal income taxes and contribute to federal Social Security. They often don't get refunds for excess withholding from their wages. Many undocumented workers don't collect Social Security benefits that they are owed. In short, the US Treasury enjoys net income from immigrants, but state and local revenues don't always cover the cost of public education, healthcare, and social services for them. The problem that requires attention is the lack of coordination between the revenues and expenditures of multiple levels of government.[15]

Addressing Economic Anxiety

Perceptions matter in politics. In fact, the word "perceptions" is a bit misleading. Perceptions are real; they can be powerful forces with consequences. What are the best responses to perceptions that immigrants cause economic harm? My answer: it's essential to take serious and visible steps to ensure that economic winners from immigration share more of their gains with groups of people, industries or occupations, or local communities or regions that may be losing out.[16]

The US immigration system has a few provisions that seem designed to share gains. Employers who hire noncitizen temporary workers must pay fees. This money funds government job training programs for citizens and lawful permanent residents, K-12 science enrichment programs, and college scholarships for low-income students in engineering, math, and computer science. Proposals in the US Congress would have broadened this sort of program, but none have become law.[17]

Examples include a bill that Congress considered in 2005. It would have required employers to recruit citizens and permanent residents, including from minority communities, for jobs before hiring H1-B temporary workers. It also would have assessed employers a 10 percent surcharge to fund job creation and training for unemployed citizens. In 2013, the Senate—but not the House—passed a bill that would have raised employers' fees if H1-B workers were at least 30 percent of their workforce.[18]

This approach calls on employers who gain most immediately from temporary workers to share some of those gains by paying fees. One limitation is that they don't cover workers in a more durable immigration status—such as lawful permanent residents in the United States. But a more basic problem is that these payments deter the hiring of the very workers who would enhance overall prosperity in the destination country. This flaw suggests that other approaches deserve some attention.

INTERNATIONAL TRADE PROMPTS questions that resemble but also differ from these questions about immigration. The consensus among economists is that international trade—like immigration—means overall economic gains for consumers, businesses, and national and global economies. But international trade can dry up a country's market for some domestic goods and hurt some workers there. These effects of international trade can produce skepticism and opposition that resemble critiques of immigration.[19]

In the United States, trade adjustment assistance has long tried to offset these effects. In 1962, President John F. Kennedy first championed US programs in their modern form. Strategies include retraining displaced workers in new skills or new jobs, and sometimes giving incentives for workers to change occupations or industries. Trade adjustment can also offer income support, unemployment insurance, wage insurance, job search and relocation allowances, and healthcare.[20]

The shortcomings of trade adjustment programs in practice have eroded the political backing that they once enjoyed. The response of organized labor changed long ago from strong support to deep skepticism. This trend exposed trade adjustment to funding cutbacks and tightened eligibility rules, especially during the Reagan presidency in the 1980s. Two decades later, the Obama administration's stimulus response to the 2008 financial crisis increased funding and expanded eligibility and benefits. But funding still remains so low that assistance has stayed inadequate.[21]

The budget for US programs to reintegrate unemployed workers into the economy is a small fraction of funding for analogous programs in other industrialized countries. As a percentage of GDP, Denmark spends twenty times more on trade adjustment than the United States, and France and Germany five times more. Even US trade adjustment programs with a successful track record, such as the Appalachian Regional Commission, remain severely underfunded.[22]

SOME MIGHT QUESTION the comparison of immigration and international trade, citing evidence that international trade has greater impact on industries and workers in the country that imports goods. As a matter of real perceptions, however, it's a political liability to make no effort to adopt something similar to trade adjustment. In doing so, it matters what the effort is called. Any program of "immigration relief" casts immigration as a burden that requires relief. It would be more helpful to view the program as one to share the prosperity that immigration fosters.

Experience with trade adjustment shows that any effective program to share gains from immigration will face formidable challenges beyond the need for adequate funding. As with international trade, sharing immigration prosperity requires first deciding who should get benefits from the program. This is challenging because the arrival of newcomers has complex effects on labor markets. As I mentioned earlier in this chapter, immigration as a driver of change is typically less significant than automation, global competition, consumer preferences, and other forces.

Research suggests that programs are effective when they go beyond narrow-gauge assistance and instead adopt a broader perspective, investing in regional infrastructure and public education. This calls for substantial funding and a bigger role for government.[23] But proposals of this sort will draw reflexive political opposition, especially if they involve more government intervention. These proposals also require time and patience to implement and to have discernable effects. Especially in the United States and other countries with a strong free market culture and traditional limits on social welfare and the role of government, it won't be easy to fund public education or training for workers and in communities that can show that immigrants are limiting their opportunities.[24]

And yet it's realistic to hope for regional investments in public education and infrastructure. Anxiety among people and communities is often rooted in worries about prosperity, especially the feeling that the future is bleak for their children. In this setting, initiatives can attract meaningful support if designed for the explicit purpose of sharing prosperity from immigration.[25]

The message matters. Consider the $25 billion or more needed for just the first phase of erecting and maintaining the US–Mexico border wall that Donald Trump championed. Opponents usually critique the wall as cruel, ineffective, and a call to hate. But they did little to emphasize that the same $25 billion could fund training and education for hundreds of thousands of US workers. Opponents didn't ask enough about the tradeoff: What's better, spending money on walls or spending money on schools?[26]

Immigration and the Historically Disadvantaged

In 1992, journalist Jack Miles published a widely read article in the *Atlantic Monthly*. It portrayed a zero-sum game, with gains by newcomers from Mexico undermining African Americans. This perspective has appeared in immigration debates for decades. After Hurricane Katrina devastated New Orleans in 2005, it was clear that rebuilding would require time, money, and workers, including many US citizens and noncitizens who traced their ancestry to Latin America. Around the same time, the federal government announced that it would suspend the enforcement of federal laws against hiring undocumented workers.[27]

For some, these developments fed a belief that Latinx workers were taking jobs from African Americans—not only that immigration hurts people who are already in a destination country, but also that immigration most severely hurts poor or working-class communities, especially the historically disadvantaged.[28] Beyond competition for jobs, research also suggests that some employers prefer Asian and Latinx workers over African Americans for some jobs. The reasons include stereotypes that Asian and Latinx employees are more willing to accept taxing work without complaint, or that African Americans are more likely to demand dignity and respect in the workplace.[29]

THE DEMOGRAPHICS OF the US Black population have evolved in the past several generations. For much of 1900s, it would have seemed natural to view Blacks in the United States as the descendants of slaves forcibly brought to the country. In 1960, only 1 percent of Blacks in the United States were foreign-born. In that era, US law admitted only a few Black immigrants into the United States.

This picture has changed as Black immigration to the United States increased since the 1960s. By 2005, 8 percent of the US Black population was foreign-born. By 2022, this had arisen to 12 percent. In six decades, Blacks of Haitian ancestry nearly quadrupled, and Blacks of Jamaican ancestry more than doubled in number. The US population of African ancestry grew substantially, with the diversity lottery a big contributing factor. These demographic changes call for care in using the terms "African Americans," "Blacks," and "immigrants."[30]

In this setting, it's natural to ask how the descendants of slaves in the United States and Black immigrants are connected in immigration policy. I'll use the term "African American" to refer to Blacks whose families have been in the United States for generations. I'll use the term "Black immigrant" for people who arrived in the past generation, typically from countries in Africa, the Caribbean, or South America. Many immigrants are Black, and many Blacks are immigrants.

Do Black immigrants undercut—or do others use them to undercut—the economic and social position of African Americans? In another arena, some observers have raised concerns that US colleges and universities achieve racial diversity by preferring the children of Black immigrants over African Americans. Narratives that highlight the success stories of Black immigrants have prompted similar reactions.[31]

In immigration policymaking, African Americans and immigrants—including Black immigrants—can find themselves pitted against each other, either of their own accord or because others hope to gain advantage by manipulating or creating tensions. A political reality is that disadvantaged communities that have been marginalized for generations are a target audience for claims that immigrants hurt people in destination countries. These claims try to influence the working class of any race or ethnicity. African Americans are natural targets for the message that immigrants have surpassed them in social and economic hierarchies.[32]

In reality, however, African Americans and other groups in the United States that have suffered discrimination have deep reasons for common cause with Black immigrants—and many other immigrants—based on their shared history as people who have been and remain marginalized, especially by racism. Measures targeting immigrants have parallels in past and present discrimination against African Americans.

The twisted cruelty of labor exploitation throughout US history includes slavery, then importing Asian labor, then tolerating or inviting Latinx workers to come outside the law—all in settings marked by systemic abuse and mistreatment. This history explains why challenges to US immigration and citizenship laws have often relied on a civil rights framework—against the same sorts of discrimination that oppressed and still oppresses African Americans.[33]

COMMON CAUSE AMONG African Americans and immigrants in the United States may depend on how issues are viewed and argued. A study published in 2018 analyzed the voting behavior of African American state legislators in US southern states. When did they vote with the majority of white legislators to support measures that reflected skepticism toward newcomers? It mattered a lot, the study found, if legislative bills were seen as economic measures or instead as anti-immigrant discrimination.[34]

In the votes covered by the study, African American legislators were more likely to join conservative whites in supporting restrictionist bills in settings that cast African Americans and newcomers as competing with each other for jobs and public resources. An example was a bill to enhance penalties for employers that hire undocumented workers. The same African American legislators were more likely to vote for measures supporting immigrants in settings that cast African Americans and immigrants as minorities who face similar discrimination or surveillance. For example, African American legislators were more likely to vote against bills to expand the immigration authority of state and local police and to impose stricter voter identification requirements.

The anti-discrimination framing was evident in the campaign against the Trump administration's efforts to end Temporary Protected Status (TPS) for several countries. The NAACP and the NAACP Legal Defense and Educational Fund brought one of the lawsuits to block the Trump decision in 2018 to end TPS for Haiti. A core allegation in the lawsuit was that ending TPS was a racist decision, as underscored by Trump's insulting comments about Haiti and what he called "shithole" countries.[35]

IF THE VIEW gains traction that racism explains measures that target immigrants, the views of African Americans may be more likely to reflect anti-discrimination framing. This would align generally with many immigrant advocacy efforts. But fundamentally, these alliances are precarious. Some political entrepreneurs will remain intent on driving a wedge between immigrants and African Americans. In this political context, the danger is a persistent belief that the government will do nothing to spread the prosperity that immigration can bring over time.

Unless economic justice for all is part of the reception of immigrants, economic anxieties will persist as fertile ground for immigration skeptics, and sometimes for bigots. Policymakers need to respond by making sure that gains from immigration are broadly shared. Otherwise, immigration policy will be a weapon for insiders who gain from immigration to win advantage over insiders who don't—a result that disrespects belonging claims.

Deeper Anxieties

I've devoted most of this chapter to economic anxiety, but not because it's necessarily the primary or fundamental source of skepticism or opposition toward immigration. It's because failure to address economic anxiety opens up space for other anxiety that's more racial, religious, or cultural.

The economy matters. Support for immigration enforcement has grown during economic downturns. When US unemployment increased in the 1990s, restrictionist attitudes gained influence in state and national policies. But this connection between the economy and immigration policy is inconsistent. Some strands of vehement opposition to immigration coalesced during the Obama presidency despite steady economic recovery from the 2008 recession, and during a period of relative prosperity after the Trump administration took office in January 2017.

More basic is that people can feel threatened by the openness and globalization that have become part of daily life throughout the world since the mid-twentieth century. In the United Kingdom, many regions that voted solidly in 2016 to leave the European Union had benefited greatly from direct EU subsidies. Polling and interviews showed that many cast ballots for Brexit against their own economic interests. They were voting against what they saw as racial, religious, or cultural threats from immigration.[36]

EVEN WHEN ANXIETY is characterized as cultural, the issues often lie deeper than the word "culture" can capture. Foreign people can be much more unsettling than foreign products. It's a sense of loss of status in society—or a general feeling that a country is no longer one's own. It's a fear of people who look different, speak strange languages, or act in unfamiliar ways. These anxieties and fears can emerge as skepticism, opposition, or hostility to some immigration and to some immigrants. These attitudes marginalize immigrants and impede the integration that's essential for respecting their belonging claims as they become insiders.[37]

Some people who are skeptical, opposed, or hostile toward newcomers are racists and religious bigots. Many are not. But economic anxiety opens up political opportunities for demagogues voicing a powerful strain of white, Christian nationalism in the United States or analogous ethnocentric views in many other countries. These demagogues have used economic anxiety as both grievance and cover to amplify prejudice grounded in discrimination and often in hate based on race, religion, ethnicity, or language. No matter what the sources of economic anxiety might be, it's easy to blame newcomers.[38]

Facts struggle to break through when prejudices are strong. The Trump administration used national security rhetoric to recycle fears unleashed by the September 11 attacks two decades earlier. As a modern first among presidents, Trump questioned lawful immigration and had "nation of immigrants" removed from the mission statement of US Citizenship and Immigration Services, the federal agency primarily responsible for deciding who comes to the United States and who becomes a US citizen.[39]

Perceptions about economics may matter more than real effects.[40] The absence of programs to share immigration prosperity will come across as neglect or indifference, allowing economic anxiety to take on outsized political importance. And that anxiety cast in economic terms can often metastasize into immigration policy that is counter-productive and punitive. Respect for the belonging claims of insiders requires efforts to even out the the economic burdens and advantages that immigration brings, and to acknowledge anxieties without pandering to racists or religious bigots.

9

What Does It Mean to Address Migration's Root Causes?

For generations, destination countries have tried to control or manage migration on their own. But it has become clear that this approach isn't sustainable. More countries have recognized—often begrudgingly—that unilateral policymaking isn't enough, and that regional cooperation is essential. This cooperation across national borders often speaks of "addressing the root causes of migration."

A good start to this inquiry is understanding that observers often treat root causes narrowly, as a matter of conditions in countries that migrants are leaving. An example is the simple notion that if things were better in another country, people who live there would have a choice to stay, and many would do so. Root causes are at least as likely to be found in destination countries. In fact, migration to the United States reflects decisions made in the United States about temporary worker programs, labor and immigration policy, immigration enforcement, and more. And in the next chapter, I'll address how destination countries have spurred migration by generating powerful forces like global inequality and climate change.[1]

In this chapter, I'll focus on root causes in countries of origin and transit. I'll explain how many of these initiatives to address root causes fall short, often becoming outsourced border control. Influencing the root causes of migration in countries of origin and transit requires rethinking transnational cooperation among countries of origin, transit, and destination. I'll also explain why encouraging remittances has distinct but complex advantages as an approach to root causes.

Making Immigration Policy Alone

An important dimension of overall ties between two or more countries is international trade. Countries can let in goods through trade, and they can let in people through migration. Both trade and migration allow countries to benefit from lower wages in less prosperous countries. It's possible to import things made at lower cost elsewhere, or to attract workers who are willing and able to come to work for higher wages. The movement of capital can enable these strategies.[2]

It's a familiar pattern to cooperate transnationally on trade but not migration. Letting in newcomers can provoke economic and cultural anxieties, so destination countries often find it less fraught in domestic politics to import goods instead. Preferring trade to migration can mean lowering trade barriers but maintaining restrictions on immigration. For example, political support in the United States for the North American Free Trade Agreement (NAFTA) and its successor, the United States–Mexico–Canada Trade Agreement, rested in part on assurances that free trade with Mexico wouldn't mean more Mexican migration.[3]

That said, some countries around the world have had agreements with other countries to arrange for work-based migration. The Bracero program sent Mexican workers to the United States from the 1940s to the 1960s. In Germany, *Gastarbeiter* programs recruited workers from southern Europe and Turkey from the 1950s into the 1970s. Many countries have programs of this sort.

In destination countries, these arrangements can raise the question of coming temporarily versus indefinitely that I explored in an earlier chapter. I focus here on a different dimension of cooperation. Especially for low-wage jobs, destination countries often don't need transnational cooperation on migration to meet their workforce needs. Even if a negotiated agreement might better reflect the interests of workers or of their countries of origin, simply offering jobs can be enough recruitment for the destination country. Some workers then come through the lawful admissions system. Other workers come outside the law.[4]

MANAGING LABOR MIGRATION on its own can reflect and reinforce a belief in a destination country that immigration policy is a core aspect of its national borders and national sovereignty. Perhaps buoyed by hubris, it can be intuitive to think that responding to migration is something that countries do by themselves.[5] But in fact, it's hard for destination countries connected to countries of origin by trade to make immigration policy alone. Trade can strengthen economic, cultural, and social ties between the two countries in ways that enhance familiarity and make migration a natural option. Trade can displace some workers who then move to seek opportunities in countries that are trading partners. For example, NAFTA made some farming in Mexico unsustainable, so many displaced farmers chose the difficult but available option to emigrate to the United States.[6]

Destination countries often turn a blind eye to these transnational dynamics and respond unilaterally to migration. Much of the response is more enforcement on the physical border and in a country's interior. In recent decades, however, migration patterns have changed. More people are moving across national borders to seek better lives. Some seek economic well-being. Others try to escape persecution, famine, war, environmental calamity, the breakdown of civil society, and other calamities. These powerful forces—combined with more available information and expanded transportation options—lead to more migration.

These trends make transnational cooperation indispensable and generate challenges and opportunities for both destination countries and for the transit countries through which migrants travel. In these fluid settings, countries of origin might gain leverage if they can influence migration. Transit countries can gain similar leverage if they can impede transit, allow transit, or become a destination country. To look at the possibilities, I'll start with countries of origin, then discuss transit countries.[7]

Addressing Root Causes in Countries of Origin

It's natural to think that economic development in countries of origin
will neutralize the forces that displace people and push them to emigrate.
The idea is that economic well-being gives people an option to stay in
their countries of origin, or to return there if they've already left. But
the effects of economic development aid on migration are more complex
than they might first appear.[8]

First, economic development can increase emigration, not reduce it.
In other words, economic well-being might not mean that more people
stay in their home countries. Aid may raise economic well-being in ways
that don't make it significantly more viable to stay, but might give people
the money they need to emigrate and reach their intended destinations.
Economic well-being can make it possible for people to follow through
on their hopes and plans.

A study by economists Michael Clemens and Hannah Postel is one of
several that cast doubt on the notion that aid to foster economic development in countries of origin will reduce migration in the short term
or medium term. Clemens and Postel concluded that "aid would need
to operate in unprecedented ways, at much higher levels of funding,
over generations, to greatly affect some of the most important plausible
drivers of emigration."[9]

Clemens and Postel were careful not to say that economic development approaches to reducing migration are bound to fail. Studies by
other economists have found that development might reduce migration. Some research suggests that aid to foster economic development
is more likely to limit emigration if the aid is used to build up healthcare, schools, and other core institutions. Programs to foster youth
employment may be more effective than efforts to increase household
wealth.[10]

According to one study, development in urban areas in countries of
origin and development aid to rural areas differ in their effects on migration. Modest economic development in rural areas may lead people to
stay there.[11] Aid to urban areas may attract rural populations to cities,
where conditions may enable emigration from the country of origin. In

urban areas, people have more contact with people and cultures outside the country. Urbanites are more likely to have access to the networks, skills, and information that allow them to leave.[12]

AS WITH ECONOMIC analyses of immigration's effects on the labor market, it's hard to take enough from these studies to tailor precise policies with confidence. Economic development aid as a response to migration can take many forms, and the effects of economic aid on the country of origin will vary. Even more fundamentally, does the entire population benefit? Or do a few people take it for private gain, with little or nothing left to change conditions in the country?

Studies suggest that economic development will reduce migration when—but only when—prosperity is achieved and sustained over time. Economic well-being will depend on urban and rural population patterns, literacy and education, morbidity and mortality, fertility rates, global economic patterns, and other factors that are challenging to assess.[13] Poverty is just one of many reasons for emigration. Just as weighty are other factors, including climate change, war, political oppression, and human rights violations. These reasons overlap with each other and with poverty to make people feel insecure. Stability and security can be at least as influential as economic development.[14]

Transit Countries

So far in this chapter, I've examined the connections between economic development and emigration from countries of origin. Countries can also be countries of transit that migrants cross to reach a country that's their destination. A country might be a country of origin, of destination, or of transit, and sometimes all three at the same time.

Mexico is an example of being all three. The United States has many newcomers from Mexico, but other US-bound migrants travel through Mexico on the way from Guatemala, Honduras, El Salvador, and also from countries around the world. For example, Chinese migrants can get visas to enter some countries in Latin America, or enter them without a visa. These migrants then head overland, north to the US–Mexico border. Some migrants end up staying in Mexico. Migrants bound for northern and western Europe pass through transit countries and may land indefinitely in one of them.[15]

In transit countries, questions about the root causes of migration apply in modified form to migrants in transit. Will they find protection or work? Might transit countries offer migrants something more attractive than moving onward? Or might transit countries keep migrants from moving onward?

AFTER THE CIVIL war in Syria displaced hundreds of thousands of migrants, Jordan agreed, in a 2016 Compact with the European Union, to issue work permits and to expand educational access for 200,000 of these migrants. In exchange, the EU pledged to give Jordan over $1.8 billion in grants and discounted loans. The EU also agreed to let products made by these workers be imported into the EU on favorable terms.[16]

The Compact rests on a sound abstract premise: that responses to forced migration should go beyond humanitarian relief and emphasize economic initiatives that are more sustainable because they don't treat migrants as charity cases. Migrants can work, become economically independent, and live fuller lives on terms that they can shape. This approach aligns with the view that I explained in an earlier chapter—that law and policy should not treat forced migrants as a fully separate category, but instead as potential full participants in the countries where they land.[17]

But the Compact's benefits have been elusive for Syrians in Jordan, especially women. Inadequate training and transportation have made it hard for workers to take available jobs. The number of work permits fell short of the Compact's 200,000 target, and Jordan lacks the factory capacity to produce goods in quantities to take full advantage of the EU's trade concessions.[18] In basic terms, the EU-Jordan Compact has failed to offer migrants the work to let them "build lives with dignity where they are," as legal scholar Jennifer Gordon has written. This is a failure to respect the humanity claims of forced migrants to live full lives.[19]

It might seem that transit countries have no choice but to take what destination countries offer, and that migrants on the move have to live with the consequences. But transit countries have bargaining leverage, precisely because they are transit countries. Some have managed to negotiate deals with destination countries that offer meaningful benefits to the transit countries and potentially to migrants, too. In 2016, the European Union secured Turkey's help in keeping migrants—especially from Syria—away from Greece and the rest of the EU. In return, Turkey received several billion Euros in monetary incentives, looser travel restrictions for Turkish citizens entering the EU, and resumption of long-stalled talks on EU membership for Turkey.[20]

One lesson may be that transit countries can get better deals than they have so far. Mexico could gain funding and win easier access for its citizens to the United States. But disparities in bargaining power between transit countries and destination countries can skew these arrangements in favor of destination countries, making them fraught with risks.[21]

DESTINATION COUNTRIES' ARRANGEMENTS with countries of origin or transit may end up as little more than outsourced border control and regional containment. This risk will arise even if the initial purpose of the arrangement was to give migrants a real option to stay in their country of origin or in a transit country.[22] Some arrangements with countries of transit and origin seem open about this focus on control and containment. Some years ago, the 2014 EU-Horn of Africa Migration Route Initiative, also known as the Khartoum Process, focused explicitly on "better managing" migration. Since then, the EU and EU member countries have entered into agreements with countries in Africa that emphasize containment. In 2024, the EU and Lebanon agreed that the EU would pay over one billion Euros to Lebanon, which in return would keep migrants from going by boat to Cyprus.[23]

Many destination countries are all too ready to have transit countries keep migrants away. Outsourcing physical borders lets destination countries sidestep many obligations that they would owe to migrants who reach the country's physical borders. This outcome is especially

tempting if the view takes hold that newcomers pose a racial or religious threat calling for stern measures. Destination countries can move
out of the spotlight, even if the other countries in the arrangement have
limited ability and willingness to assess claims for protection. The EU
lets the Turkish government decide if migrants are refugees who qualify for asylum. The Trump administration tried in 2019 to shunt asylum
seekers on the US southern border to Guatemala for decisions in their
cases.[24]

These arrangements may incentivize a repressive transit country
regime "to violate the rights of refugees and migrants in order to demon-
strate its capacity to control migration," as one study put it. Turkey's
collaboration with the EU has strengthened President Tayyip Erdoğan.
Funding for the police and military can entrench authoritarian governments in transit countries—heightening the oppression and human
rights violations that can drive emigration in the first place.[25]

THE CORE FACT is a tension between two approaches. On the one hand,
funding for outsourced border control can have an immediate visible
effect by curtailing migration. But outsourced border control may have
little long-term effect on migration, given the powerful forces that propel it. On the other hand, economic development and other improved
conditions in countries of origin and transit will take time to limit
migration—and may even increase it in the short term.

What seems to work at first will likely not work in the long run. What
might work in the long run will likely not seem to work at first. Without quick results, it's tempting for destination countries to give up on
addressing root causes and on promoting development, and instead to
divert funding to police and military for containment in countries of
transit and origin.[26]

In those scenarios, it's likely that national borders will disrespect the
humanity claims of migrants, for example through harsh enforcement
without giving them a chance to seek asylum. Migrants won't have a fair
process to decide whether they should be allowed to stay. Even worse,
letting destination countries outsource border control diminishes the
transparency and accountability that are essential to detect and remedy

problems. A related risk is disrespect for the belonging claims of insiders in destination countries who are close to the people who are targets of outsourced border control.

Finding Ways Forward

The need for time and patience means that initiatives to influence migration in the long term are politically fragile. This is true for both transit countries and countries of origin. The long timeline can undermine sustained efforts to address root causes. Some observers or decision-makers might conclude that addressing root causes is doomed to failure, but I think that's unduly pessimistic. Only time will tell if measures that address root causes will be effective. Progress will be slow, but it's important to understand that if sustained efforts had started a generation ago to improve conditions in many countries of origin and transit, many migrants would be far less desperate than they are today.

Confronting the tough issues ahead won't be easy and will take time, but without resolve and a roadmap, the task will slip into impossibility. The key is not letting the quest for short-term payoffs like rapid decreases in the number of migrants eclipse far-sighted policy. Well-resourced destinations like the United States and most European Union countries need to emphasize long-term goals and reject demands for quick reductions in migration.

IT'S HELPFUL TO examine the Marshall Plan after World War II. It was vital to European renewal and to long-term global prosperity and security. It gave people a choice to rebuild their lives without leaving their home countries. But the Marshall Plan wasn't cast or intended as a migration management tool. It was a broader nation-building and region-building effort. It strove not just for economic prosperity but also for security and political stability in Europe.[27]

This nation-building goal may have let the Marshall Plan's champions treat it as a long-term initiative. The framing generated the patience that allowed it, over time, to influence migration along with reaching other

outcomes. In contrast, programs that characterize economic development aid as a response to migration imply the use of migration-focused
metrics for success. This mindset may keep economic development
efforts from being in place long enough to affect migration. Casting
development aid as migration management can make the turn toward
border control hard to resist.[28]

WHAT THE MARSHALL Plan accomplished suggests a way to interpret
improved economic conditions and political stability in South Korea,
Poland, and Ireland. In the 1990s and 2000s, many migrants returned
to these countries from the United States. Mexico may be showing the
start of some similar effects, with the number of Mexican migrants to the
United States declining over the past decade.[29]

The European Union offers another example. Its origins go back to a
period of cooperative reconstruction after the devastation of World War
II. The exigencies of that era allowed freedom of movement to become a
bedrock premise, despite concerns about large-scale migration among its
member countries. In 1986 the EU expanded to include Spain and Portugal, prompting unease in some existing EU countries about migration
from Spain and Portugal to the rest of the EU. But substantial migration didn't happen. EU development funds directed toward Spain and
Portugal helped give people reasons to stay home or to return there.

Recent tensions within the EU may mean that lessons from the EU
experience are unclear or cautionary. Starting in the early 1990s, the
entry of some former Soviet bloc countries widened economic and political differences within the EU.[30] But some lessons emerge. One is that
economic differences need not be equalized, but enough must be done to
give people a real choice to stay at home or return. Another lesson is that
economic development must go hand in hand with efforts to guarantee
political stability, personal security, and human rights.

A third lesson is that lawful migration pathways are crucial. When
the EU expanded to include Spain and Portugal, membership in the EU
assured their citizens that they could move freely within the EU in the
future. Without that assurance, they might have migrated then, in case

they couldn't later. This effect seems paradoxical, but true. Opening up lawful pathways allows people in countries of origin or transit to assess more rationally when it makes sense for them to become migrants. This, too, is a way of addressing migration's root causes.[31]

As with all references to specific historical examples, reasonable questions can arise about how useful they are. The Marshall Plan and the European Union did not involve the sort of racial and religious dynamics that might arise in applying its lessons to migration from Africa or the Middle East. The lessons of Korea, Poland, and Ireland will be less directly useful in countries not poised to make an economic leap. The reasons for people to migrate from Spain and Portugal to the rest of the EU were moderate enough that being able to migrate later deterred migrating immediately. These differences make the current challenge daunting, but not impossible. It's easy to overlook how many migration flows stopped or slowed in the past generation in ways that once seemed speculative or impossible at an earlier time. It's essential to shift from emphasizing how these examples might differ from current circumstances to asking: How can today's migration situations become more like these examples?

Remittances

Thinking about economic development and lawful migration pathways combine to suggest another way forward—remittances, the money that migrants send back to their communities, typically to family members. Worldwide remittances are triple what governments devote to economic development aid. Remittances would be even more substantial if the fees that financial institutions charge to send money were lower. These funds enable much more than short-term spending. They help educate children, build houses, start and grow businesses, and more.[32]

In broad concept, remittances function as a form of aid devoted to economic development; they support support investment as well as consumption. Remittances are private transfers of money that generally stay under the control of individuals, families, and other small-scale decision-makers. Migrants decide where to direct them. The communities that benefit directly are likely to be the points of origin for migrants who send remittances.[33]

One feature of remittances is their potential to entrench inequalities that limit who can migrate in the first place. Remittances flow back to the migrants' families or communities, and so privilege the people close to the migrants who were able to make the journey across national borders and find employment. These migrants may be more likely to be young men. Moreover, the likelihood of their success in destination countries may depend on discriminatory filters like race or religion.

An alternative is to send economic aid to the government or other institutions in the country of origin. In theory, political leaders and bureaucrats might be better positioned to coordinate the overall positive impact of economic aid, in contrast to remittances. But in practice, official efforts might be inefficient or counterproductive. When funds arrive as remittances to private parties, political leaders and bureaucrats in central or regional governments have less influence. This minimizes the impact of any corruption. Relatedly, remittances minimize the risk of reinforcing autocratic regimes and make it more likely that funds go toward the country's broader well-being.[34]

A BASIC PARADOX comes with viewing remittances as a way to address the root causes of migration. Remittances can lead to changes in a country of origin that give people a meaningful choice to stay home or return there. But remittances assume migration. Some people have to migrate before their remittances can give others the choice to stay or return.[35]

This relationship between the short term and the long term resembles the time dimension of economic development. Ways to stabilize migration in the long term may increase migration in the short term. Similarly, letting in more workers in statuses that are initially temporary can increase remittances, improve conditions, and in the long run give more people a choice to stay home or to return.

Any emphasis on remittances requires flexibility in managing lawful migration pathways. The conceptual foundation is the spectrum from temporary to indefinite that I explored in an earlier chapter.[36] The key point there was that admitting people temporarily at first is consistent with some of them becoming insiders who should be able to stay indefinitely. People may stay temporarily, or migrate back and forth, or go back to countries of origin. All options allow remittances in ways that give people in countries of origin some real choices to return or not to migrate in the first place. As with other ways to address root causes, remittances can reduce the need to implement national borders in ways that disrespect persuasive humanity clams.

Transparency and Accountability

Addressing the root causes of migration in countries of origin or transit is beset with interwoven uncertainties. One is the core challenge of identifying what might work, and what does or doesn't work. Another challenge is sustaining efforts that are promising. And assessing success or failure is difficult because political, economic, and demographic circumstances will evolve. Only time can tell how long unsettled conditions will persist in Syria, Central America, Ukraine, Venezuela, Afghanistan, or other troubled areas. It's impossible to say in advance. As of 2023, an estimated 25 million people had been in exile for at least five years after leaving their home countries. Migrants' stories may become local integration where they end up, onward movement, or return to their country of origin.[37]

Given the need for sustained efforts, the institutional arrangements and values that shape decision-making will matter. This is true not only for a country's unilateral decisions but also for transnational arrangements. Transparency and accountability in decision-making are crucial. Possibilities—and tradeoffs—include broader participation and greater public scrutiny in working transnationally on migration.

Directly affected migrants have often been shut out of negotiations between destination countries and countries of origin or transit.

For example, the EU-Jordan Compact emerged from a limited circle of negotiators without international organizations and agencies, nongovernmental organizations, or the migrants themselves.[38] As initiatives move from negotiations through design to implementation, the influence of the private sector may become more pronounced and yet more opaque, making transparency more vital.

KEY TO TRANSPARENCY is disclosure, which is essential for assessing how any arrangement affects people. The question—and the challenge—is how to achieve the best balance of transparency and productive negotiations.[39] On the one hand, transparency may mean making sure that the same degree of public scrutiny that usually applies to government decisions would also apply to transnational arrangements. From this perspective, it's troubling to insulate these transnational arrangements. On the other hand, public exposure may impede agreement. On balance, governments may sometimes need to limit publicity, but they shouldn't be immune from scrutiny.[40]

Essential is thinking in two dimensions. One is to make sure that these arrangements respect the humanity claims of all and the belonging claims of insiders. The other is the dimension of time, and in particular thinking for the long term and adopting immigration policy that will shape a better future—not necessarily for today, but more importantly for future generations. The results of sound decisions about immigration policy may take decades to become evident. But consider this: if policymakers had made those decisions a generation ago, many people all over the world wouldn't be suffering as much as they are today.

10

What's the Big Picture?

So far, I've tried to answer nine questions that are fundamental to immigration policy. I hope that I've acknowledged each question's complexity. Every question is linked to several others, perhaps to all of the others. The combination sheds new light and is crucial for seeing the path ahead. I've relied primarily on examples from the United States, but the lessons apply in many countries. In this final chapter, I'll use some examples from earlier chapters to answer a tenth question: What's the big picture? In other words, what bedrock themes cross-cut the previous nine? Here are four.

First, what injustices do national borders conceal? Second, how should immigration decisions be made? Which people and institutions should have decision-making power, and what processes should they adopt? Third, how should immigration policy reflect history, geography, economics, and other broad perspectives on the ties among countries? Fourth, what should be the role of immigration policy in larger social, cultural, and political terms to rectify injustices in the world? The answers combine to frame the big picture for responses to human migration.

What Injustices Can National Borders Conceal?

I wrote in an earlier chapter that borders have benefits. Borders are the foundation of belonging, and with belonging can come identity, culture, agency, and pride. But borders can also be the Achilles heel of a fair and just society. Borders can mask injustices by creating lawless zones where the principles of justice that apply inside borders—if imperfectly—apply weakly if at all. Borders can create zones where injustices go undetected or unremedied, or are normalized and legitimated, and so aren't seen as injustices at all. In these ways, borders often allow dominant elements in a society to maintain power in spite of demographic and other changes.[1]

Some injustices involve treatment that no one should endure. This idea protects every person no matter what their ties may be to the country that inflicts harm. This is why I've used the term humanity claims. Examples include cruel enforcement, denial of protection from threats, unfair decision-making, and racial or religious discrimination. Other injustices reflect disrespect for claims by some people—I've called them insiders because they are part of communities in the country. I've called these belonging claims. These claims reflect a sense of justice derived from the nation-state and national legal systems. In the United States, this perspective taps into the history of civil rights struggles of marginalized people to claim their rightful place in national society.

Both types of claims have one thing in common. Both express doubt about legal categories. To say that someone or something is illegal can mask the real issues, make decision-making opaque, and immunize those responsible for disrespecting humanity claims or belonging claims. Mechanical reliance on legal categories leads to lawlessness and undermines the rule of law. Being outside a country's borders or having no ties to a country doesn't mean that it can impose its will with impunity. People who are in a country without lawful status can still be insiders with persuasive claims based on belonging.

The injustices that national borders conceal or normalize can take many forms. I've given examples, and I'll add a few more here. Some are in the open, such as deportation of long-time residents. Well known, but often disregarded, is that many newcomers—with or without lawful status—become part of communities in the country. Much less visible is the history of unauthorized migration, especially acquiescence, tolerance, and even invitation to people to come outside the law, and to live and work precariously.

Other injustices are concealed in how decisions are made. In the United States, the undocumented are vulnerable to discretionary enforcement by immigration agencies and by law enforcement in general. These decisions may disrespect humanity claims or belonging claims. So might enforcement at private hands. Employers can take advantage of undocumented workers through wage theft or other abuses. Border vigilantes may believe that their behavior will escape serious examination.

WHO SUFFERS WHEN borders and immigration policy disrespect humanity claims or belonging claims? Patterns have evolved over time and vary by country and region. In the United States, a through-line has been race and racism. Discrimination by race was explicit for much of US history in the form of racial bars to immigration and citizenship.

More recently, racial discrimination has been more subtle and harder to correct. An example is the illegalization of workers of color who are vital to the economy but don't have access to lawful status because work-based admissions categories are too narrow for the needs of the economy. It's essential to be vigilant about discrimination, and to ensure the transparency and accountability needed to make vigilance effective.

Religion is another axis of injustice that national borders can normalize. In the United States, fears emerged in the mid-1800s that Catholics would overrun Protestant America. These reactions laid the foundation in that era for hostility toward Irish and German newcomers. Much more recently, laws and policies after September 11, 2001—in the United States and elsewhere—used religion to distinguish people to fear from people to welcome.

The Trump administration's 2017 Muslim ban was another example of religious bias for which national borders were a tool to legitimate. It—and post-9/11 measures before it—disrespected the belonging claims of insiders who were marginalized by these laws and policies, as well as the humanity claims of all people—some insiders, some not—against discrimination, cruel enforcement, unfair process, and denial of protection from harm.[2]

CLOSELY RELATED TO race and religion in the United States was the use of immigration policy—by letting in newcomers from Europe—to conquer and settle territory by displacing, dispossessing, and exterminating Native peoples. This meant subordinating the people whose history on the land made them insiders before anyone else was. Discussions of immigration to the United States typically omit this topic.[3]

It's no accident that US citizenship laws were slow to recognize Native Americans as citizens. This use of national borders in the form of citizenship laws reflects these words from legal scholar Alexander Bickel: "It has always been easier, it always will be easier, to think of someone as a noncitizen than to decide that he is a nonperson."[4]

Gender is an additional arena where national borders have been instruments for injustice. For a long period of US history, laws governing citizenship treated women as appendages of their husbands. Women who were US citizens lost their citizenship if they married men who were citizens of other countries. In 1922, Congress repealed this general rule, but it survived in an explicitly racist form. If women married men from Asian countries, they continued to lose their US citizenship until 1931.[5]

Another theme is economic class. Destination countries have often let in newcomers without sharing with people who are already there the prosperity that immigration brings over time. All too often, the displacements that immigrants can cause in the short term go unaddressed. This, too, is injustice that borders can mask and legitimate.

I've listed only some of the ways that national borders have enabled, normalized, concealed, and seemed to legitimate injustice. My general point is broader: that national borders have privileged some insiders over others whose belonging claims have been disrespected. And national borders have denied the respect for humanity claims that all people have. Borders can make disrespect and subordination seem normal. I'm not saying that all humanity claims and belonging claims are persuasive. Some won't be, and so some challenges to aspects of national borders will not succeed. But without taking them seriously, it's impossible to know.

How Should Immigration Policy Be Made?

Much of this book has probed the substance of immigration policy. What about the process of making immigration policy? In earlier chapters, I've examined many aspects of process. I'll now explore how these process issues are connected to each other.

One dimension is reaching fair and accurate results in implementing national borders through immigration laws and policies. A second dimension involves discretion in decision-making to provide flexibility, while also ensuring that discretion doesn't enable or mask outcomes that are problematic. Closely related is a third dimension: ensuring that decision-makers don't delegate enforcement authority in ways that enable or mask problems. All three dimensions call for adequate funding, which in turn demands public commitment to immigration policy that respects humanity claims and belonging claims.

Fair and Accurate Results

Decision-making in the immigration system now suffers from the basic problem of unfair or inaccurate results in cases that decide the fates of individuals and families. Many decisions require assessment of intricate facts and application of a complicated set of immigration statutes, regulations, and policies. Fairness and accuracy often require research into complex law.

It's hard to be confident in the results in cases unless the system is structured to overcome practical obstacles to fairness and accuracy. It's essential to have a minimum process for all people—not only for insiders, but also for people with humanity claims such as forced migrants seeking protection. In the United States, noncitizens facing deportation have no constitutional right to a lawyer who is appointed for them. But fair and accurate results typically require the involvement of a lawyer with the expertise to investigate, research, advise, and represent. Outcomes must not vary by financial means. Equally troubling are outcomes skewed by imprisonment, which inherently hampers communication with lawyers and can wear down people to the point that they abandon their legal cases.[6]

As another aspect of process, government decision-makers must have all available relevant evidence. They must be impartial not just by minimizing explicit bias, but also by collectively reflecting a broad range of professional and personal backgrounds. The time available for cases to be presented and decided must be long enough to allow full airing, but not so long that the duration of the process itself is punishment. Review on appeal is indispensable not just to bolster confidence in the initial decision, but also to ensure that outcomes are broadly consistent among agency decision-makers, immigration judges, and federal court judges.[7]

Discretion

Government immigration decisions involve different types of discretion—all ways to manage the large gap between the letter of the law and widespread violations in practice. One type of discretion allocates resources to enforce against some types of violations or violators, while putting less priority on others. Other discretionary decisions have produced legislation that imposes heavier penalties on some violations than others, or requires detention in some cases but not others. Discretion is also part of decisions to select people to stop, arrest, detain, and deport.[8]

Respect for humanity claims and belonging claims puts limits on these exercises of discretion. A key goal should be to shield discretionary decisions from the prejudices and inconsistencies of enforcement personnel. Crucial is the publication of enforcement priorities, as has become standard in the United States. The Trump administration deviated from this pattern with an executive order that purported to do away with priorities, but in fact let agency personnel set their own priorities out of public view.[9]

Countering rogue decisions by agency personnel that disregard published priorities requires systems to grant relief based on general criteria. In the United States, Deferred Action for Childhood Arrivals (DACA) and Temporary Protected Status (TPS) are examples. Both programs regularized the exercise of discretion by allowing noncitizens to apply and by shifting decisions from an enforcement agency's field offices to a central office of an agency handling immigration-related services.[10]

WHEN GOVERNMENT OFFICIALS apply immigration law to individual cases, discretion plays a large role that requires monitoring. Legal rules create categories using generalizations that are based on a combination of stereotypes and data. For example, discretionary relief might allow release from detention. Or discretionary relief can allow relief from deportation altogether and grant durable immigration status to a noncitizen. In the United States, the principal scheme for this type of discretionary relief has two basic defects. One is limited eligibility to apply. Requirements include a long period of physical presence or residence, a severe form of hardship, and a close relative who is a US citizen or lawful permanent resident.[11]

Many noncitizens don't meet these requirements even though they are part of communities in the country and therefore have belonging claims. Moreover, the system for deciding cases lacks guardrails sufficient to ensure that decisions are consistent with each other and don't reflect improper bias. To respect humanity claims and belonging claims, discretionary relief requires expanded eligibility, publicized standards for granting or denying relief, and review by another decision-maker to ensure consistency in outcomes. These measures would work toward essential transparency and accountability.

Delegation

I've just explained the need for processes designed to reach fair and accurate results, and to allow discretion but with transparency and accountability. The goal is making sure that improper decisions don't escape detection and remedy. Working toward this goal is more daunting when governments delegate decision-making authority to a broader set of actors.

In the United States, the federal government has delegated some immigration enforcement authority to states and localities. State and local police use federal databases in ways that check an arrestee's immigration status, and the federal government has deputized some state and local agencies to be involved in federal enforcement. The federal government asks state and local jails and prisons to hand over, for possible deportation, noncitizens who finish their criminal sentences.[12]

Immigration federalism refers to the limits of state and local immigration authority in the United States. If the federal government doesn't delegate, many questions turn on the doctrine of federal preemption, which invalidates state and local laws and policies if they address an area of law that the federal government has occupied, or if those laws or policies are inconsistent with federal law. On the surface, the issue is what separates federal turf from state and local turf. The traditional approach is to decide if a law or policy is a matter of immigration law affecting matters of admission and expulsion, and thus under exclusive federal control, or if it instead addresses another area of law and thus involves immigration law only indirectly.[13]

From the perspective of respect for humanity claims and belonging claims, however, it's essential to give careful thought to the scope of state and local authority. This is true both when the federal government delegates authority and when state and local initiatives are not preempted. State and local involvement in enforcement has sometimes targeted communities based on race or ethnicity and abused enforcement discretion. In such situations, state and local involvement in immigration enforcement is likely to limit the transparency and accountability that are needed to ensure respect for humanity claims or belonging claims. Similar but often heightened concerns arise with enforcement by private actors, including prison companies and vigilantes.[14]

I'VE JUST EXPLAINED why federal preemption should invalidate state and local laws and policies when preemption can prevent concealed discrimination. Does this reasoning apply to the state and local laws and policies that are sometimes called sanctuary measures? For example, states and localities might decline to cooperate with federal enforcement. Or they might try to integrate noncitizens regardless of their immigration status. Sanctuary measures are controversial. But they are much less likely to enable undetected and unremedied discrimination or other improper discretionary decisions. This is a meaningful difference.[15]

For enforcement decisions, people stopped by state and local police frequently have some evidence of racial or ethnic profiling, but it's often not enough to establish improper discrimination in court. The reason is that the US Constitution requires that they prove the intent to discriminate. Given this requirement, federal preemption addresses the risk that state or local discrimination will avoid direct challenge and so escape detection and remedy for lack of proven intent. Preemption does this by shifting to prevention—by withholding authority from state or local actors who might abuse it.

For an area where state and local laws and policies don't run the same risk of undetected or unremedied harm, compare a state law that lets undocumented resident students pay the same lower in-state tuition at public colleges and universities as resident US citizens. Undocumented students will pay less, so citizen students may have to pay slightly more, depending on how the college or university covers the cost of granting the in-state discount. But this harm is much more diffuse than discrimination in enforcement. In fact, federal courts have consistently ruled that this sort of harm isn't enough to give citizen students standing to sue in federal court at all. This means that preemption is appropriate to prevent the improper exercise of enforcement discretion, but the same rationale doesn't apply to preempt many sanctuary measures.[16]

How Should History Matter?

The next big-picture theme is the role of history and similarly broad ways of understanding the context for responses to human migration. This theme also connects ideas and examples from throughout this book. The task is to see how immigration policy reflects history, geography, economics, and the like. It's a matter of degree, as several examples combine to show.

Consider the treatment of forced migrants displaced by armed conflict in which the destination country played a major role. The United States was at the center of wars involving Vietnam and Afghanistan, which ended with many people forced to leave those countries. Some had worked with the US military or US government agencies. Many had not, but victorious adversaries still targeted them for their perceived ties to the United States. In this sort of situation, denying protection from harm that someone would face in the country would be especially troubling disrespect of a core humanity claim. This is especially true where, as here, the United States was part of these conflicts.[17]

NEXT, CONSIDER PROGRAMS to offer lawful status to some undocumented people in the United States. Here the relevance of history is strong, but it's not as direct as with forced migrants from Vietnam or Afghanistan. The large undocumented population reflects US immigration and labor policies. The lawful migration pathways have been too restricted to meet the economy's workforce needs.[18]

Congress could have expanded these pathways and taken steps to offset the economic anxiety that newcomers might generate. But Congress never did either of these things in a meaningful way. US policy acquiesced in migrants coming to work without papers. The historical pattern has been reliance on undocumented workers, many of them nonwhite. This gap between law on the books and law in action created a system of selective admissions, selective enforcement, and vast discretion. The US economy benefitted from a cheap, flexible, and disposable workforce—taking advantage of their labor but denying them respect.

Over time, the system illegalized millions of newcomers. Regardless of how decision-makers should address unauthorized migration in the future, the response must respect the belonging claims of many of today's undocumented noncitizen residents by offering lawful status and a path to citizenship. The conceptual foundation combines history, geography, and economics in a way that's direct enough to make legalization a targeted response to a specific major problem.

AS CONNECTIONS BETWEEN history and policy get more indirect, it likely becomes harder to convince people that history matters. An example is the federal law that criminalizes unlawful entry and reentry into the United States. This law's original supporters in 1929 wanted to preserve the purity of the country's Anglo-Saxon stock against what they saw as contamination with Mexican blood. In 1952 Congress adopted the Immigration and Nationality Act, which reenacted and consolidated federal immigration laws, including the unlawful entry and reentry provision. But its supporters weren't as open with their racism as the advocates for the original version in 1929 had been.[19]

Unlawful entry and reentry are among the most frequently charged federal crimes. In 2022, a noncitizen charged with unlawful reentry asked a federal district court to dismiss the case against him because of the statute's racist origins. The court agreed and did just that. But the federal court of appeals reversed, citing the absence of express racism in 1952 and treating reenactment in that year as if it had been entirely new. In spite of evidence that the 1952 Congress saw Mexico as a source of cheap, flexible, and disposable workers, the explicit racism in 1929 didn't seem to matter anymore.[20]

I recognize that the connection between the past and the present in the context of unlawful entry and reentry statutes might seem less direct than it is in the context of people fleeing conflicts in which a country has been involved very recently, and also less direct than with people who are undocumented as a consequence of US immigration and labor policy from the early twentieth century to the present. This looser connection can lead some to think that history should have a much smaller role in decision-making today.[21]

But race and racism have been central in US history to admitting noncitizens, granting citizenship, and enforcing immigration laws. Many routine approaches to enforcement have explicitly racist origins. The system built on this foundation remains, even if it typically adopts more neutral language. The issues and challenges lie deeper than the initial step of excavating lost history.[22]

Many people turn a blind eye to history. I've had many conversations about immigration policy with people who acknowledge historical injustices. But many of them honestly think that they bear no responsibility, or that they needn't be part of any response. They say that they didn't benefit from wrongdoing in past generations, even wrongdoing by their own government—or that even if they benefited, they did nothing wrong. More generally, the 2020s have seen the rise of movements to suppress the teaching of history, perhaps out of fear that knowledge of the past is a subversive force.[23]

What's missing now—urgently needed but elusive—is forthright public conversation about laws with racist origins. Perhaps statutes should remain and be enforced in spite of such origins. Another approach could be shifting to civil penalties, to treat unlawful entry and reentry no more severely than overstaying the terms of admission. For related reasons, Congress could repeal current criminal penalties if they punish some immigration law violators more severely because of their country of origin, and so are likely to disrespect humanity claims and belonging claims.

ANOTHER EXAMPLE OF history pertinent to immigration policy involves the relationship between Mexico and the United States. Much of the sizeable population of Mexican ancestry in the United States traces its lineage back to people who lived on US soil when it was part of Mexico—before the end of the Mexican–American War and the Treaty of Guadalupe Hidalgo in 1848. Others are part of families who came in the generations since. Should US policy rely on the history of the US–Mexico relationship to treat migrants from Mexico more favorably than migrants from Guatemala, Haiti, Senegal, China, or elsewhere?[24]

When Congress repealed the national origins admissions system in 1965, it ended an explicit type of official racial discrimination. Around that time, Congress moved toward formal equality for Mexican migration. The limits on the number of immigrants from any one country applied to every country worldwide, including Mexico. These decisions disregarded historical ties between Mexico and the United States.[25]

The result was to limit lawful admissions from Mexico and contribute to what became a large unauthorized population, largely from Mexico. Treating countries in superficially equal ways can mask treatment that's unequal. This disrespects the humanity claims of migrants against racial discrimination and the belonging claims of insiders of Mexican ancestry.

One reasonable response would take this history into account and loosen the per-country limit that forces many Mexican immigrants to wait longer than immigrants from almost any other country. Another would be to rework the United States–Mexico–Canada Trade Agreement to allow more trade-related migration from Mexico. Or the United States could broaden a full range of lawful migration pathways for people from Mexico. As with the issue of criminalizing unlawful entry and reentry, this is an overdue conversation that needs to take place, not be avoided.[26]

What Should Immigration Policy Do?

I've just explored areas of immigration policy with connections to contexts shaped by history. These connections vary from immediate and direct to ones that seem less direct. It's a spectrum that raises profound questions about the relationship of the past to the making of policy now and into the future.

The historian Tony Judt once wrote that a nation must first remember the past before it can move beyond and forget it. It's a formidable challenge. To put Judt's idea differently, it's essential to reject amnesia, to look soberly at history, and to search the past for lessons to guide the way forward in deciding how to respond to migration.[27]

How far does this logic go? Answering this question should start by acknowledging a spectrum. Closer to one end, in the examples I've just given, connections bind current choices among law and policy options tightly to history. Closer to the other end, connections are looser—though in many ways no less real.[28] Prior US involvement in much of Latin America was exploitative and helped create the conditions that displace millions of migrants today. European colonization of Africa created the conditions—often brutal—that are reflected in today's migration patterns. From this perspective, national borders and immigration policy are the consequences of racism, colonialism, imperialism, and exploitative capitalism.[29]

This history prompts challenging questions. How much should immigration policy rectify past injustices among countries? How much should immigration policy offset the effects of colonization, economic exploitation, and trade and investment patterns that have led to global inequality and created the conditions for migration today? How much should immigration policy become a place for repair, reparations, and progress toward regional or global justice?[30]

IN ANSWERING THESE questions, what's the right balance between the realistic and the utopian? This brings me back to what I wrote in the Introduction about a realistic utopia. It will be hard to convince enough people to adopt a universal restorative purpose as a general guide for immigration policy. It will be even harder to convince people today that they should accept some blame or guilt for the past.

But it's realistic—and possible—to start with specific aspects of policy that are tied closely to history. An essential element is to make sure that acknowledging history is not about blame or guilt for the past. Blame and guilt are distractions from the hard work at hand. Instead, it's a more straightforward process of putting current issues in historical context. The examples that I've offered—legalization, penalties, and Mexican migration to the United States—are opportunities for a strong and attainable start. Analogous goals are realistic in other settings elsewhere in the world.

I concede that imposing the constraints of the realistic on an attempt to strive toward utopia can lead to moments of profound frustration. But expecting immigration law and policy to be the vehicle for correcting all historical injustices imposes a burden that no single area of law or policy can bear. Being so absolutist about national borders that the only arguments are for all or for nothing is likely to lead to nothing. What matters is seeing and taking steps along the way. Some of those steps should allow history to start in small ways to influence policy, and then to take bigger steps over time. That's a compass for finding the best balance between the realistic and the utopian for any given day or any given decision.

Conclusion

Moving Forward

I wrote in the Introduction that this book reflects conversations about immigration policy that I've had with myself and a great many other people over the years. I've come to believe that a utopian vision of immigration policy is an essential compass. But it's also crucial to understand what is realistic and sustainable in light of the political constraints that come with nation-states and national borders.

It's natural to ask: Will borders ever respect the humanity claims of all and the belonging claims of insiders? If it's a stark choice between yes and no, then maybe the answer is no. But as I wrote in the Introduction, I'm not predicting that national borders will ever be ideal. That's not the right way to see the challenge. Instead, this book is a guide to everyone's evaluation and decision-making every single day about any law, policy, practice, decision, or attitude that affects migration and migrants.

And so my emphasis is on identifying and taking steps forward. In the United States, this incremental approach generated the ideas, laws, and policies of Temporary Protected Status, DACA, cancellation of removal, parole, and other meaningful steps that led in turn to other meaningful steps. It's realistic to make a difference for millions of people all over the world, even if complete success seems elusive.

THE CURRENT MOMENT in world history and politics reflects great divergence between the realities of human migration and the responses of governments. Overdue is a fundamental shift in prevailing habits of thought and decision-making. It's especially important to move beyond false choices. Too many choices in the making of immigration policy try to divide up complex realities into simple categories.

For example: When people move across national borders, are they refugees or migrants? Are they moving lawfully or unlawfully? Are they moving for family or for work? Are they staying temporarily or indefinitely? Categories can be convenient and comfortable. But they can easily oversimplify and even deceive—not just people in powerful positions, but also everyday people whose thoughts and feelings matter. Categories might seem to clarify, but in fact they can obscure the facts, conceal injustice, then enable cruelty and silence voices that need to be heard.

Also overdue is correcting a basic flaw in how US policymakers make many decisions that affect other countries and shape the US relationship with countries throughout the world. Historically, these policymakers pursued their geopolitical or economic goals, often indifferent to the effects on people who would become migrants. Nothing ever required them to write migration impact statements, but that may have been a pivotal omission.

I'VE WRITTEN THIS book because I believe that many people and many decision-makers are open to understanding borders and immigration policy in broader terms. Instead of reacting to migration after it happens, they can anticipate migration trends and lay the foundation for political support. Above all, decision-makers can give people real and meaningful choices about how to make the best of their lives in ways that might or might not involve migration. It's crucial to evaluate what can respond realistically but consistent with fairness and justice to migration and to the political forces that migration generates in a world of nation-states. This combination of the realistic and the utopian can identify the concrete steps forward.

Many people, working in their own settings around the world, need to help reform the implementation of national borders, shifting immigration policy in the right direction. This journey requires the faith that comes from knowing what milestones lie ahead, even if when we'll reach them remains uncertain. Change won't happen overnight. But we can do much better than we're doing now.

Endnotes

INTRODUCTION

1. See John Rawls, The Law of Peoples 11 (1999). See also Joseph H. Carens, The Ethics of Immigration 299–300 (2014); Ruud Koopmans, Die Asyl-Lotterie: Eine Bilanz der Flüchtlingspolitik von 2015 bis zum Ukraine-Krieg (2023).

CHAPTER 1

1. See Ayelet Shachar, The Birthright Lottery: Citizenship and Global Inequality (2009).
2. See Linda Bosniak, Territorial Presence as a Ground for Claims: Some Reflections, 14 Etikk i Praksis: Nordic J. Appl. Ethics 53, 54–61 (2020). For settings where different rules apply, see United States v. Montoya de Hernandez, 473 U.S. 531 (1985); United States v. Ramsey, 431 U.S. 606 (1977); United States v. Martinez-Fuerte, 428 U.S. 543 (1976).
3. United Nations General Assembly, The Universal Declaration of Human Rights (UDHR), G.A. Res. 217 (III) A (1948).
4. On prolonged detention, see Johnson v. Arteaga-Martinez, 142 S. Ct. 1827 (2022). On border wall injuries, see Kate Morrisey, UC San Diego Trauma Doctors Say Migrant Injuries, Deaths Rose as Border Wall Grew Taller, L.A. Times, Apr. 29, 2022. On detention conditions, see Zolan Kanno-Youngs, Squalid Conditions at Border Detention Centers, Government Report Finds, N.Y. Times, July 2, 2019. On family separation, see Jacob Soboroff, Separated: Inside an American Tragedy (2020).
5. For pioneering work, see Bosniak, Territorial Presence; Linda Bosniak; Being Here: Ethical Territoriality and the Rights of Immigrants, 8 Theoretical Inquiries in Law 389 (2007). On territorial personhood in court decisions, see Hiroshi Motomura, Americans in Waiting: The Lost Story of Immigration and Citizenship in the United States 63–79 (2006).
6. On integration, see Hiroshi Motomura, Immigration Outside the Law 89–96 (2014); Motomura, Americans in Waiting, at 160–73.
7. On civic solidarity, see Sarah Song, What Does It Mean To Be an American?, 138 (2) Daedalus 31, 31–32 (2009).
8. See Gabriel J. Chin & Anna Ratner, The End of California's Anti-Asian Alien Land Law: A Case Study in Reparations and Transitional Justice, 29 Asian Am. L.J. 17, 18–31 (2022).
9. See Fla. Stat. Ann. § 692.201–.205; Edgar Chen, With New "Alien Land Laws" Asian Immigrants Are Once Again Targeted by Real Estate Bans, Just Security, May 26, 2023.
10. See Motomura, Immigration Outside the Law, at 178–80.
11. See Motomura, Americans in Waiting, at 148–49.

CHAPTER 2

1. See, e.g., Meghan Benton, Lawrence Huang, Jeanne Batalova & Tino Tirado, The State of Global Mobility in the Aftermath of the COVID-19 Pandemic (Migration Policy Inst. 2024); World Migration Report (Marie McAuliffe & Linda Adhiambo Oucho eds., Int'l Org. for Migration 2024).

2. See, e.g., Carens, The Ethics of Immigration, at 194–99; David Miller, Strangers in Our Midst: The Political Philosophy of Immigration 78 (2016); Michael Walzer, Spheres of Justice: A Defense of Pluralism and Equality 48–51 (1983).

3. See Colin Yeo, Refugee Law 4–11 (2022); James Hathaway & Michelle Foster, The Law of Refugee Status (2d ed. 2014); Guy Goodwin-Gill & Jane McAdam, The Refugee in International Law (4th ed. 2021).

4. See Convention Relating to the Status of Refugees, July 28, 1951, 189 U.N.T.S. 137 (entered into force Apr. 22, 1954).

5. See Tony Judt, Postwar: A History of Europe Since 1945, at 28–31 (2005); Katy Long, From Refugee to Migrant? Labor Mobility's Protection Potential 4–5 (Migration Policy Inst. 2015).

6. See INA §§ 208(b)(1)(A), 209(b), 8 U.S.C. §§1158(b)(1)(A), 1159(b); INA § 316(a), 8 U.S.C. § 1427(a).

7. See INA § 101(a)(42), 8 U.S.C. § 1151(a)(42); INA § 208(b)(1)(A), 8 U.S.C. § 1158(b)(1)(A). On ineligibility based on crimes, see the Convention Relating to the Status of Refugees art. 33(2), July 28, 1951, 189 U.N.T.S. 137 (entered into force Apr. 22, 1954); INA §§ 208(b)(2)(A)(ii), (iii), 241(b)(3)(B)(ii), (iii), 8 U.S.C. §§ 1158(b)(2)(A)(ii), (iii), 1231(b)(3)(B)(ii), (iii). On ineligibility based on past participation in persecution or national security, see INA §§ 208(b)(2)(A)(i), (iv), 241(b)(3)(B)(i), (iv), 8 U.S.C. §§ 1158(b)(2)(A)(iv), 1231(b)(3)(B)(i), (iv).

8. See Vincent Chetail, Are Refugee Rights Human Rights? An Unorthodox Questioning of the Relations Between Refugee Law and Human Rights Law, in Human Rights and Immigration 19, 23–24, 39–40 (Ruth Rubio-Marín ed., 2014). Refugee protection before World War II focused more on economic inclusion. See Rieko Karatani, How History Separated Refugee and Migrant Regimes: In Search of Their Institutional Origins, 17 Int'l J. Refugee L. 517, 541 (2005); Katy Long, When Refugees Stopped Being Migrants: Movement, Labour and Humanitarian Protection, 1 Migr. Stud. 4, 10, 13–21 (2013).

9. See INA § 241(b)(3), 8 U.S.C. § 1231(b)(3) (on withholding of removal); United Nations Convention Against Torture and Other Cruel, Inhuman or Degrading Treatment or Punishment, Dec. 10, 1984, 1465 U.N.T.S. 85.

10. See INA § 209(a), 8 U.S.C. § 1159(a) (adjustment to lawful permanent residence).

11. On the worldwide population that may qualify, see U.N. High Commissioner for Refugees, Mid-Year Trends, at 12–16 (2023); U.N. High Commissioner for Refugees, Global Trends: Forced Displacement in 2022, at 2 (2023). For annual determinations, see Presidential Determination on Refugee Admissions for Fiscal Year 2024, Pres. Determination No. 2023-13, 88 Fed. Reg. 73521 (2023); Presidential Determination on Refugee Admissions for Fiscal Year 2020, Pres. Determination No. 2020-04, 84 Fed. Reg. 65903 (2019); ;U.S. Annual Refugee Resettlement Ceilings and Number of Refugees Admitted, 1980–Present (Migration Policy Inst. 2023).

12. On the refugee-migrant binary, see Rebecca Hamlin, Crossing: How We Label and React to People on the Move 1–9 (2021); Heaven Crawley & Dimitris Skleparis, Refugees,

Migrants, Neither, Both: Categorical Fetishism and the Politics of Bounding in Europe's "Migration Crisis," 44 J. Ethnic & Migr. Studs. 48, 50–52 (2018); Elizabeth Keyes, Unconventional Refugees, 67 Am. U. L. Rev. 89, 138–47 (2017).

13. On not viewing refugee recognition as a matter of right, see T. Alexander Aleinikoff & Leah Zamore, The Arc of Protection: Reforming the International Refugee Regime 17–20 (2019); David A. Martin, Reforming Asylum Adjudication: On Navigating the Coast of Bohemia, 138 U. Pa. L. Rev. 1247, 1266–70 (1990).

14. See Middle East and North Africa: Migrants Deaths and Disappearances in 2023 (Int'l Org. for Migration 2024); US-Mexico Border World's Deadliest Migration Land Route (Missing Migrants Project 2023).

15. See Displacement Overview (Norwegian Refugee Council 2023); Alan Bersin, Nate Bruggeman & Ben Rohrbaugh, Migration at the U.S.-Mexico Border: A Challenge Decades in the Making 30 (Migration Policy Inst. 2024).

16. See Bersin, Bruggeman & Rohrbaugh, at 30. On keeping forced migrants away, see David Scott FitzGerald, Refuge Beyond Reach: How Rich Democracies Repel Asylum Seekers (2019).

17. See FitzGerald, Refuge Beyond Reach, at 41–251; Chetail, at 23–24, 51–52; T. Alexander Aleinikoff & David Owen, Refugee Protection: "Here" or "There," Migr. Studies 464, 465 (2022).

18. See Sale v. Haitian Ctrs. Council, 509 U.S. 155, 158–65 (1993); Müge Kinacioglu, Militarized Governance of Migration in the Mediterranean, 6 Int'l Affairs 2423 (2023); Ayelet Shachar, The Shifting Border: Legal Cartographies of Migration and Mobility 75–82 (2020).

19. See Aliens Subject to a Bar on Entry Under Certain Presidential Proclamations; Procedures for Protection Claims, 83 Fed. Reg. 55934 (2018); Presidential Proclamation Addressing Mass Migration Through the Southern Border of the United States, Proclamation No. 9822, 83 Fed. Reg. 57661 (2018).

20. See Aristide R. Zolberg, A Nation by Design: Immigration Policy in the Fashioning of America 110–13, 264–67 (2006).

21. See Common Implementation Plan for the Pact on Migration and Asylum, Council Com. (EU) No 251/2024 of the European Parliament and Council of June 12, 2024; European Council Press Release, EU-Turkey Statement (Nov. 29, 2015); European Council Press Release, EU-Turkey Statement (Mar. 18, 2016); Elizabeth Collett, The Paradox of the EU-Turkey Refugee Deal (Migration Policy Inst. 2016) Fact Sheet: EU-Libya Relations, Eur. Union External Action (Nov. 9, 2018); Kate Hooper, European Leaders Pursue Migration Deals with North African Countries, Sparking Concerns about Human Costs (Migration Policy Inst. 2017); Andrew Macaskill & Sachin Ravikumar, New UK Leader Starmer Declares Rwanda Deportation Plan "Dead and Buried," Reuters, July 10, 2024. On safe third countries, see Safe Third Country Agreement Canada-U.S., Dec. 5, 2002, T.I.A.S. No. 04-1229; Dublin II Regulation: Council Reg. (EC) No 343/2003 of 18 Feb. 2003; Dublin III Regulation, Reg. (EU) No 604/2013 of the European Parliament and Council, June 26, 2013.

22. See INA §§ 272, 273, 8 U.S.C. §§ 1322, 1323.

23. See 42 U.S.C. § 265; Centers for Disease Control & Prevention, US Dep't of Health & Human Servs., Order Suspending the Right to Introduce Certain Persons from Countries Where a Quarantinable Communicable Disease Exists, 85 Fed. Reg. 65806 (2020); US Att'y. Gen., Attorney General Sessions Delivers Remarks Regarding the Immigration

Enforcement Actions of the Trump Administration (May 7, 2018); Ms. L. v. U.S. Immigration & Customs Enf't, 310 F. Supp. 3d 1133, 1136–37 (S.D. Cal. 2018) (on family separation).

24. For restrictions on access, see Yeo, at 14–15. See also INA § 235(b)(1), 8 U.S.C. § 1225(b)(1) (expedited removal).

25. See 42 U.S.C. § 265; Memorandum from Kirstjen M. Nielsen, Sec'y, US Dep't of Homeland Sec., to L. Francis Cissna, Dir., US Citizenship & Immigration Servs., Kevin K. McAleenan, Comm'r, US Customs & Border Prot., Ronald D. Vitiello, Deputy Dir. & Senior Official Performing the Duties of Dir., US Immigration & Customs Enf't, on Policy Guidance for Implementation of the Migrant Prot. Protocols (Jan. 25, 2019).

26. See US Dep't of Homeland Security, Guidance Regarding the Court-Ordered Reimplementation of the Migrant Protection Protocols (Memorandum from R. Silvers to CBP, ICE, CIS) (Dec. 2, 2021); US Dep't of Homeland Security, Termination of the Migrant Protection Protocols (Memorandum from A. Mayorkas to ICE, CBP, CIS Directors) (Oct. 29, 2021); Centers for Disease Control & Prevention, US Dep't of Health & Human Servs., Public Health Determination and Order Regarding the Right to Introduce Certain Persons From Countries Where a Quarantinable Communicable Disease Exists (2022).

27. See, e.g., Circumvention of Lawful Pathways, 88 Fed. Reg. 31314 (2023); Proclamation No. 10773, 89 Fed. Reg. 111 (2024).

28. See Matter of A–B–, 27 I & N Dec. 316, 317, 320–23, 345 n.12 (A.G. 2018); vacated, Matter of A–B–, 28 I & N Dec. 307 (A.G. 2021).

29. See Vivian Salama & Alex Leary, Trump Says Southern-Border Asylum Seekers are Running a "Scam," Wall St. J., April 5, 2019.

30. See Hamlin, at 1–24; Keyes, at 138–47 (on the limitations of the current Convention-based protection regime). This division is reflected in two separate international agreements: the Global Compact for Safe, Orderly, and Regular Migration and the Global Compact on Refugees. See Jennifer Gordon, The International Governance of Refugee Work: Reflections on the Jordan Compact, 1 Global Public Policy & Governance 239 (2021).

31. See Convention Governing the Specific Aspects of Refugee Problems in Africa, Art. I(2), 1001 U.N.T.S. 45 (entered into force June 20, 1974).

32. See Cartagena Declaration on Refugees, Colloquium on the International Protection of Refugees in Central America, Mexico and Panama, Nov. 22, 1984. On limited application of the African Convention and the Cartagena Declaration, see Yeo, at 39–53.

33. See Jane McAdam & Sanjula Weerasinghe, Climate Change and Human Movement, in Climate Change, Justice and Human Rights 27 (David Ismangil, Karen van der Schaaf & Lars van Troost, eds. 2020); Eric A. Posner, Climate Change and Human Rights, in Climate Change, Justice and Human Rights, at 21.

34. See Directive 2004/83/EU; Directive 2011/95/EU; Maryellen Fullerton, Temporary Protection in the United States and the European Union: Same Words, Vastly Different Meanings, 9 U. Penn. J. L. & Public Affairs 1 (2024).

35. See Yeo, at 56–59.

36. See INA § 244, 8 U.S.C. § 1254a. For an example of DED, see Deferred Enforced Departure for Certain Palestinians, Exec. Mem. 10773, 89 Fed. Reg. 12743 (2024).

37. See US Citizenship & Immigr. Servs., Temporary Protected Status.

38. See Muzaffar Chishti, Jessica Bolter & Sarah Pierce, Tens of Thousands in United States Face Uncertain Future, as Temporary Protected Status Deadlines Loom (Migration Policy Inst. 2017).

39. See Council Implementing Decision (EU) 2024/1836 (2024); Council Implementing Decision No 382/2022 (2022); Council Directive 2001/55/EC, arts. 13(2), 14 (2001); Fullerton, at 34-47.

40. See Implementation of a Parole Process for Haitians, 88 Fed. Reg. 1243 (2023); Implementation of a Parole Process for Nicaraguans, 88 Fed. Reg. 1255 (2023); Implementation of a Parole Process for Venezuelans, 87 Fed. Reg. 63507 (2022); Implementation of the Uniting for Ukraine Parole Process, 87 Fed. Reg. 25040 (2022); Implementation of a Change to the Parole Process for Cubans, 88 Fed. Reg. 26329 (2023). Several Republican-led states sued the federal government to block this program as beyond executive branch authority, and this lawsuit is ongoing. See Texas v. DHS, 2024 WL 1021068 (S.D. Tex. March 8, 2024), appeal pending.

41. See Protracted Refugee Situations Explained (U.N. High Commissioner for Refugees 2020).

42. See Aleinikoff & Zamore, at 21–23; Keyes, at 137–47; Denise Gilman, Making Protection Unexceptional: A Reconceptualization of the U.S. Asylum System, 55 Loy. U. Chi. L.J. 1, 66–70 (2023).

43. See David J. Cantor, Environment, Mobility, and International Law: A New Approach in the Americas, 21 Chicago J. Int'l L. 263 (2021) ("The legal literature on the environment-mobility nexus largely overlooks how wider immigration law could address international mobility challenges linked to adverse environmental conditions").

44. On the need to include development actors in decisions about refugee reception, see Susan Fratzke & Camille Le Coz, Strengthening Refugee Protection in Low- and Middle-Income Countries 8–13 (Migration Policy Inst. 2019). On economic opportunities for forced migrants in several African countries, see Alexander Betts, The Wealth of Refugees: How Displaced People Can Build Economies (2021).

45. See Yeo, at 23–24; Diana Kay & Robert Miles, Refugees or Migrant Workers? The Case of the European Volunteer Workers in Britain (1946–1951), 1 J. Ref. Stud., 214–16, 233 (1988). On Germany, see Jessica Bither & Astrid Ziebarth, Creating Legal Pathways to Reduce Irregular Migration? What We Can Learn From Germany's "Western Balkan Regulation" 10 (Migration Strategy Group 2018); Migration, Integration, Asylum: Political Developments in Germany 2016, at 24 (Federal Office for Migration and Refugees 2017).

46. See Gesetz über den Aufenthalt, die Erwerbstätigkeit und die Integration von Ausländern im Bundesgebiet § 104(c) (Chancen-Aufenthaltsrecht).

47. See Chapter 1.

48. See Cathryn Costello & Michelle Foster, (Some) Refugees Welcome: When Is Differentiating Between Refugees Unlawful Discrimination?, 22 Int'l J. Discrim. & L. 244 (2022) (using refugee definition to argue for protection against racial and other discrimination).

CHAPTER 3

1. See Leila Kawar, Contesting Immigration Policy in Court: Legal Activism and Its Radiating Effects in the United States and France 73–77 (2015); Saskia Bonjour, Speaking of

Rights: The Influence of Law and Courts on the Making of Family Migration Policies in Germany, 28 L. & Pol'y 328, 340–45 (2016).

2. See Peter Kolchin, American Slavery, 1619–1877, at 3–4 (rev. ed. 2003); Dred Scott v. Sandford, 60 U.S. 393, 454 (1857).

3. See U.S. Const. amend. XIV, § 1; United States v. Wong Kim Ark, 169 U.S. 649 (1898). On citizenship for Native peoples, see U.S. Pub. L. 68–175, 43 Stat. 253 (1924); U.S. Pub. L. 49–105, 24 Stat. 388 (1897); INA § 301(b), 8 U.S.C. § 1401(b).

4. See Act of Mar. 26, 1790, ch. 3, § 1, Stat. 103, 103 (1790); Act of July 14, 1870, ch. 254, § 7, 16 Stat. 254, 256 (1870). The Nationality Act of 1940 made eligible "races indigenous to the Western Hemisphere." Eligibility expanded to immigrants from China in 1943, and India and the Philippines in 1946. See Nationality Act of 1940, ch. 3, § 303, 54 Stat. 1137, 1140; Act of Dec. 17, 1943, ch. 344, § 3, 57 Stat. 600, 601; Act of July 2, 1946, ch. 534, § 303(a)(1), 60 Stat. 416, 416 (1946); Act of June 27, 1952, Pub. L. No. 82-414, ch. 477, § 311, 66 Stat. 163, 239 (ending race, sex, and marital status restrictions).

5. See U.S. Pub. L. 43–141; 18 Stat. 477 (1875); Act of May 6, 1882, ch. 126, § 14, 22 Stat. 58, 61 (1882); Act of Apr. 27, 1904, ch. 1630, § 5, 33 Stat. 392, 428 (1904); repealed by Act of Dec. 17, 1943, ch. 344, § 1, 57 Stat. 600, 600 (1943). On the 1875 law, see Kerry Abrams, Polygamy, Prostitution, and the Federalization of Immigration Law, 105 Colum. L. Rev. 641, 690–715 (2005).

6. On the plenary power doctrine, see Hiroshi Motomura, Immigration Law After a Century of Plenary Power: Phantom Constitutional Norms and Statutory Interpretation, 100 Yale L.J. 545 (1990); Hiroshi Motomura, The Curious Evolution of Immigration Law: Procedural Surrogates for Substantive Constitutional Rights, 92 Colum. L. Rev. 1625 (1992); Stephen H. Legomsky, Immigration Law and the Principle of Plenary Congressional Power, 1984 Sup. Ct. Rev. 255.

7. See Chae Chan Ping v. United States, 130 U.S. 581, 598, 606 (1889); Fong Yue Ting v. United States, 149 U.S. 698, 729–30 (1893).

8. See 12 Stat. 392, 392 (1862) (Homestead Act); Motomura, Americans in Waiting, at 115–19, 193.

9. See Executive Order 589 (1907); Roger Daniels, The Politics of Prejudice: The Anti-Japanese Movement in California and the Struggle for Japanese Exclusion 31–45 (1962); Motomura, Americans in Waiting, at 31–32.

10. See Act of Feb. 5, 1917, ch. 29, § 3, 39 Stat. 874, 876.

11. See US Congress, Immigration Commission, 1 Abstracts and Reports of the Immigration Commission, 24, 47–48 (1911).

12. See Act of May 19, 1921, ch. 8, §§ 2(a)(6), 3, 42 Stat. 5, 5–7; Act of May 26, 1924, ch. 190, § 5, 43 Stat. 153, 155; Motomura, Americans in Waiting, at 126–33.

13. See US Immigration Comm'n, Abstract of the Report on Japanese and Other Immigrant Races in the Pacific Coast and Rocky Mountain States, in Reports of the Immigration Commission: Abstracts of Reports of the Immigration Commission with Conclusions and Recommendations and Views of the Minority, S. Doc. No. 61-747, at 690–91 (3d Sess. 1911). For the statutes, see INA §§ 275, 276, 8 U.S.C. §§ 1325, 1326. On the legislative background, see Brief for Professors Kelly Lytle-Hernandez, Ingrid Eagly, and Mae Ngai as Amici Curiae Supporting Respondent, United States v. Palomar-Santiago, 141 S. Ct. 1615 (2021).

14. See Act of Dec. 17, 1943, ch. 344, § 1, 57 Stat. 600, 600 (repealing Chinese exclusion); Act of June 27, 1952, Pub. L. No. 82-414, ch. 477, § 311, 66 Stat. 163, 239 (codified at

INA § 311, 8 U.S.C. § 1422 (ending race, sex, and marital restrictions); Act of Oct. 3, 1965, Pub. L. No. 89-236 § 2(a), 79 Stat. 911, 911–12 (1965).

15. See Civil Rights Act of 1964, Pub. L. No. 88-352, 78 Stat. 241; Voting Rights Act of 1965, Pub. L. No. 89-110, 79 Stat. 437. On civil rights and immigration in this period, see Mary L. Dudziak, Cold War Civil Rights: Race and the Image of American Democracy 152–248 (2000). On demographics, see U.S. Immigrant Population and Share Over Time, 1850–Present (Migration Policy Inst. 2024).

16. 403 U.S. 365 (1971). See Graham, Brief for Appellees at 10.

17. See Graham, 403 U.S. at 372.

18. See In re Griffiths, 413 U.S. 717 (1973); Sugarman v. Dougall, 413 U.S. 634 (1973). See also Lau v. Nichols, 414 U.S. 563, 564–69 (requiring English-language instruction for meaningful participation in public education); Kawar, at 47–64.

19. On the unauthorized population in the 1970s, see Arthur F. Corwin, The Numbers Game: Estimates of Illegal Aliens in the United States, 1970–81, 45 L. & Contemp. Probs. 223 (1983); Joyce Vialet, Illegal/Undocumented Aliens 1 (Cong. Res. Serv. 1984); Joyce Vialet, Illegal/Undocumented Aliens 1 (Cong. Res. Serv. 1981); Joyce Vialet, Illegal Aliens: Analysis and Background 1 (Cong. Res. Serv. 1977). For changes in law, see INA § 202(a)(2), 8 U.S.C. § 1152(a)(2) (2012); Immigration and Nationality Act Amendments of 1976, H.R. Rep. No. 94-1553, 94th Cong., 2d Sess. 1976, at 1–4 (1976); S. Rep. No. 89-748, 89th Cong., 1st Sess. 1965, at 17–18; see also Act of Oct. 3, 1965, Pub. L. No. 89-236, §§ 8, 21(e), 79 Stat. 911, 916, 921; Act of Oct. 20, 1976, Pub. L. 94-571, § 3, 90 Stat. 2703 (amending INA); Act of Oct. 5, 1978, Pub. L. No. 95-412, 92 Stat. 907 (1978); Act of Mar. 17, 1980, Pub. L. No. 96-212, 94 Stat. 102 (1980). On the end of the Bracero program, see David Fitzgerald, A Nation of Emigrants: How Mexico Manages Its Migration 48–55 (2009). On migration patterns, see Fitzgerald, Nation of Emigrants, at 55–56; Motomura, Immigration Outside the Law, at 45–46; Douglas S. Massey, Luin Goldring & Jorge Durand, Continuities in Transnational Migration: An Analysis of Nineteen Mexican Communities, 99 Am. J. Soc. 1492, 1496–1503 (1994).

20. See Plyler v. Doe, 457 U.S. 202 (1982).

21. See Tex. Educ. Code Ann. § 21.031 (1981); Brown v. Board of Educ. of Topeka, 347 U.S. 483, 483 (1954); Plyler, 457 U.S. at 205–06.

22. On the significance of Plyler and the plaintiffs' strategy, see Kawar, at 51–55; Motomura, Immigration Outside the Law, at 1–12; Michael A. Olivas, No Undocumented Child Left Behind: *Plyler* v. *Doe* and the Education of Undocumented Schoolchildren 7–33 (2012).

23. See Foley v. Connelie, 435 U.S. 291, 296 (1978); Ambach v. Norwick, 441 U.S. 1589, 1593 (1979); Cabell v. Chavez-Salido, 454 U.S. 432, 445 (1982). On the rights of lawful permanent residents from Graham to the early 1980s, see Allison Brownell Tirres, The Unfinished Revolution for Immigrant Civil Rights, 25 U. Pa. J. Con'l Law 846 (2023).

24. See J. David Goodman, Texas Governor Ready to Challenge Schooling of Migrant Children, N.Y. Times, May 5, 2022.

25. On equality as a rule of law value, see Paul Gowder, The Rule of Law in the Real World 6–7 (2016).

26. 459 U.S. 21 (1982).

27. On procedural due process, see Mathews v. Eldridge, 424 U.S. 319 (1976).

28. See Muzaffar Chishti & Kathleen Bush-Joseph, In the Twilight Zone: Record Number of U.S. Immigrants Are in Limbo Statuses (Migration Policy Inst. 2023).

29. 576 U.S. 86 (2015).
30. 585 U.S. 667 (2018).
31. 114 S. Ct. 1812 (2024).
32. See Hiroshi Motomura, Whose Immigration Law?: Citizens, Aliens, and the Constitution, 97 Colum. L. Rev. 1567, 1572 (1997); Hiroshi Motomura, Whose Alien Nation?: Two Models of Constitutional Immigration Law, 94 Mich. L. Rev. 1927, 1946–50 (1996). See also Kawar, at 55–59 (on civil rights-based court challenges to US treatment of Haitian asylum seekers); Christopher Sebastian Parker, Status Threat: Moving the Right Further to the Rights, 150 (2) Daedalus 56, 60 (2021) (on references to "real Americans").
33. See The White House, Fact Sheet: Biden-Harris Administration Announces New Border Enforcement Actions (Jan. 5, 2023).
34. Quoted in Dexter Filkins, Biden's Dilemma at the Border, The New Yorker, June 12, 2023.
35. See Maggie Astor, Trump Doubles Down on Migrants "Poisoning" the Country, N.Y. Times, Mar. 17, 2024; Eugene Scott, Trump's Most Insulting—and Violent—Language is Often Reserved for Immigrants, Wash. Post, Oct. 2, 2019; Ben Zimmer, Where Does Trump's "Invasion" Rhetoric Come From?, Atlantic, Aug. 6, 2019; Katie Rogers & Nicholas Fandos, Trump Tells Congresswomen to "Go Back" to the Countries They Came From, N.Y. Times, July 14, 2019; Alexandra Hutzler, Texas Gov. Greg Abbott Says End of Title 42 Will Bring "Total Chaos," ABC News, Dec. 18, 2022; Nicholas Confessore, For Whites Sensing Decline, Donald Trump Unleashes Words of Resistance, N.Y. Times, July 13, 2016.

CHAPTER 4

1. On family-based immigration generally, see Hiroshi Motomura, The Family and Immigration: A Roadmap for the Ruritanian Lawmaker, 43 Am. J. Comp. L. 511 (1995).
2. See INA § 201(b)(2)(A)(i), 8 U.S.C. § 1152(b)(2)(A)(i) (on immediate relatives); INA § 101(b)(1), 8 U.S.C. § 1101(b)(1) (on children). On the US Constitution and same-sex marriages, see Obergefell v. Hodges, 576 U.S. 644 (2015).
3. See INA § 203(a), 8 U.S.C. § 1153(a) (on family categories). On waiting periods, see U.S. Dep't of State, Visa Bulletin; David Bier, 8.3 Million Relatives of U.S. Citizens & Legal Residents Awaited Green Cards in 2022 (Cato Inst. 2023).
4. See INA § 203(d), 8 U.S.C. § 1153(d) (on spouses and children); INA § 212(h), 8 U.S.C. § 1182(h) (on waivers); INA § 240A, 8 U.S.C. § 1229b (on family ties as a shield).
5. See U.S. Dep't of State, Visa Bulletin; 88 Fed. Reg. 43591 (2023) (Colombia); 88 Fed. Reg. 43601 (2023) (Honduras); 88 Fed. Reg. 43611 (2023) (El Salvador); 88 Fed. Reg. 43581 (2023) (Guatemala).
6. See INS v. Hector, 479 U.S. 85 (1986).
7. See INA § 101(b)(1)(G)(ii), 8 U.S.C. § 1101(b)(1)(G)(ii).
8. See Chapter 3.
9. See Chapter 6.
10. See Alan Hyde, The Law and Economics of Family Unification, 28 Geo. Immigr. L.J. 355 (2014); Jimy M. Sanders & Victor Nee, Immigrant Self-Employment: The Family as Social Capital and the Value of Human Capital, 61 Am. Soc. Rev. 231 (1996).

11. On innovation, see Alex Nowrasteh, Expand Legal Immigration to Boost the Economy (Cato Inst. 2021); Robert Krol, Effects of Immigration on Entrepreneurship and Innovation, 41 Cato J. 551 (2021). On essential workers, see Ryan Allen, Jose D. Pacas & Zoe Martens, Immigrant Legal Status among Essential Frontline Workers in the United States during the COVID-19 Pandemic Era. 57 Int. Migr. Rev. 521 (2023); Miriam Jordan, Farmworkers, Mostly Undocumented, Become "Essential" During Pandemic, N.Y. Times, Apr. 2, 2020.

12. See Chapter 8.

13. On categories and needs, see Damien Cave & Christopher F. Schuetze, Contending with the Pandemic, Wealthy Nations Wage Global Battle for Migrants, N.Y. Times, Nov. 23, 2021. On education, see INA § 203(b)(1), (2), (3), 8 U.S.C. § 1153(b)(1), (2), (3). On labor market tests, see INA § 212(a)(5), 8 U.S.C. § 1182(a)(5), see Office of the Inspector Gen., U.S. Dep't of Labor, 81 Semiannual Report to Congress 11 (2019); Ben A. Rissing & Emilio J. Castilla, House of Green Cards: Statistical or Preference-Based Inequality in the Employment of Foreign Nationals, 79 Am. Soc. Rev. 1226 (2014).

14. On this numerical limit, see INA § 203(b)(1), (2), (3), 8 U.S.C. § 1153(b)(1), (2), (3). On the number of spouses and children in employment categories, see Dep't of Homeland Sec., 2022 Yearbook of Immigration Statistics tbl. 7, 20–22 (2023). On waiting periods, see U.S. Dep't of State, Visa Bulletin.

15. See INA § 214(g)(1), 8 U.S.C. § 1184(g)(1); US Citizenship & Immigr. Services, H–1B Electronic Registration Process.

16. See Robert Warren, An Analysis of the US Undocumented Population Since 2011 and Estimates of the Undocumented Population for 2021, 11 J. Migr. & Human Sec. 279 (2023); Jeffrey S. Passel & Jens Manuel Krogstad, What We Know About Unauthorized Immigrants Living in the U.S. (Pew Research Ctr. 2023); Jennifer Van Hook, Julia Gelatt & Ariel G. Ruiz Soto, A Turning Point for the Unauthorized Immigrant Population in the United States 7 (Migration Policy Inst. 2023).

17. See Chapter 6.

18. On US investor visas, see INA § 203(b)(5), 8 U.S.C. § 1153(b)(5). See also Jelena Dzankic, Rollback of "Golden Passports" Shows Their Elusive Shine (Migration Policy Inst. 2022); Kristin Surak, Millionaire Mobility and the Sale of Citizenship, 47 J. Ethnic & Migr. Stud. 166 (2021).

19. See Select Commission on Immigration and Refugee Policy, Final Report 336 (1981) (Hesburgh, dissenting) ("the rich should not be able to buy their way into this country"). On criticism, see Muzaffar Chishti & Faye Hipsman, Controversial EB-5 Immigrant Investor Program Faces Possibility of Overhaul (Migration Policy Inst. 2016). On fraud, see Katharine Q. Seelye, Fraud Charges Mar a Plan to Aid a Struggling Vermont Region, N.Y. Times, May 10, 2016; SEC and USCIS Issues Investor Alert Advising of Investment Scams that Exploit Immigrant Investor Program, 90 Interpreter Releases 1992 (2013).

20. The Trump ban is Proclamation No. 9645, Enhancing Vetting Capabilities and Processes for Detecting Attempted Entry Into the United States by Terrorists or Other Public-Safety Threats, 82 Fed. Reg. 45161 (2017). Inadmissibility grounds are in INA § 212(a), 8 U.S.C. § 1182(a).

21. See Trump v. Hawaii, 585 U.S. 667 (2018); Chapter 3.

22. See INA § 202(a)(2), 8 U.S.C. § 1153(a)(2); US Dep't of State, Visa Bulletin.

23. See INA § 203(c), 8 U.S.C. § 1153(c); Anna Law, The Diversity Visa Lottery: A Cycle of Unintended Consequences in United States Immigration Policy, 21 J. Am. Ethnic Hist. 3–5, 18 (2002).
24. See Chapter 10.

CHAPTER 5

1. See INA § 101(a)(15)(H), 8 U.S.C. § 1101(a)(15)(H).
2. See INA § 101(a)(15)(L), 8 U.S.C. § 1101(a)(15)(L) (L nonimmigrants); INA § 101(a)(15)(E)(i), (ii), 8 U.S.C. § 1101(a)(15)(E)(i), (ii) (E nonimmigrants).
3. See 8 C.F.R. § 214.2(f)(5).
4. For an overview, see Chishti & Bush-Joseph.
5. See INA § 212(d)(5)(A), 8 U.S.C. § 1182(d)(5)(A).
6. See Chapter 2.
7. See Adam B. Cox & Cristina M. Rodriguez, The President and Immigration Law 49–72 (2020).
8. See Implementation of the Uniting for Ukraine Parole Process, 87 Fed. Reg. 25040 (2022); Dep't of Homeland Sec., DHS Announces Upcoming Re-parole Process for Afghan Nationals, May 5, 2023; Muzaffar Chishti & Jessica Bolter, Welcoming Afghans and Ukrainians to the United States: A Case in Similarities and Contrasts (Migration Policy Inst. 2022). See also 87 Fed. Reg. 63507 (2022) (Venezuela); 88 Fed. Reg. 26329 (2023) (Cuba); 88 Fed. Reg. 1255 (2023) (Nicaragua); 88 Fed. Reg. 1243 (2023) (Haiti); 88 Fed. Reg. 43611 (2023) (El Salvador); 88 Fed. Reg. 43601 (2023) (Honduras); 88 Fed. Reg. 43591 (2023) (Colombia); 88 Fed. Reg. 43581 (2023) (Guatemala).
9. See INA § 244, 8 U.S.C. § 1254a.
10. See INA § 212(d)(5), 8 U.S.C. § 1182(d)(5); Cox & Rodriguez, The President and Immigration Law, at 67–68.
11. See President Barack Obama, Remarks by the President on Immigration (June 15, 2012); Memorandum from Janet Napolitano, Sec'y of Homeland Sec., on Exercising Prosecutorial Discretion with Respect to Individuals Who Came to The United States as Children 1 (June 15, 2012); Deferred Action for Childhood Arrivals (DACA): By the Numbers 7 (Cong. Res. Serv. 2021).
12. See Texas v. DHS, 2024 WL 1021068 (S.D. Tex. March 8, 2024), appeal pending. On the history, see Cox & Rodriguez, The President and Immigration Law, at 54–73.
13. On the Trump attempts to rescind, see 83 Fed. Reg. 26074 (2018) (Honduras); 82 Fed. Reg. 47228 (2017) (Sudan); 83 Fed. Reg. 2654 (2018) (El Salvador); 83 Fed. Reg. 2648 (2018) (Haiti); 82 Fed. Reg. 59636 (2017) (Nicaragua), 83 Fed. Reg. 23705 (2018) (Nepal). See also Ramos v. Nielsen, 336 F. Supp. 3d 1075 (N.D. Cal. 2018), appeal dismissed, 2023 WL 4363667 (June 29, 2023).
14. See US Dep't of Homeland Sec., Deferred Action for Childhood Arrivals, 87 Fed. Reg. 53152 (2022). On the legal foundation, see Hiroshi Motomura, The President's Dilemma: Executive Authority, Enforcement, and the Rule of Law in Immigration Law, 55 Washburn L.J. 1, 11–14 (2015). The US Supreme Court invalidated the rescission in Dep't of Homeland Sec. v. Regents of the Univ. of California, 591 U.S. 1 (2020).
15. See Hiroshi Motomura, The Many Meanings of In-Between, in L'Expérience de la mobilité de l'Antiquité à nos jours, entre précarité et confiance 83 (Claudia Moatti & Emmanuelle Chevreau eds., 2021).

16. See Adam B. Cox & Eric A. Posner, The Second-Order Structure of Immigration Law, 59 Stan. L. Rev. 809 (2007). See also Hiroshi Motomura, Choosing Immigrants, Making Citizens, 59 Stan. L. Rev. 857 (2007).

17. See F. Ray Marshall, Economic Factors Influencing the International Migration of Workers, in Views across the Border 163, 169 (Stanley R. Ross ed., 1978).

18. See Chapter 6, Chapter 7.

19. See Chapter 9.

20. See Daniel Costa, As the H-2B Visa Program Grows, the Need for Reforms That Protect Workers Is Greater Than Ever (Economic Policy Inst. 2022); H-2B Worker Protection Task Force, Strengthening Protections for H-2B Temporary Workers (White House 2023). See also Close to Slavery: Guestworker Programs in the United States (Southern Poverty L. Ctr. 2013).

21. See Valeria Ottonelli & Tiziana Torresi, The Right Not to Stay: Justice in Migration, the Liberal Democratic State, and the Case of Temporary Migration Projects 43–64, 89–141 (2023); Martin Ruhs, The Price of Rights: Regulating International Labor Migration 136–38 (2013); Sarah Song, Immigration and Democracy 154–55 (2018).

22. See Nicola Cantore & Massimiliano Calì, The Impact of Temporary Migration on Source Countries, 49 Int'l Migr. Rev. 697 (2015).

23. See Chapter 8.

24. Max Frisch, Überfremdung I, in Schweiz als Heimat? 219, 219 (Walter Obschlager ed., 1990) (my translation).

25. See Michael J. Piore, Birds of Passage Birds of Passage: Migrant Labor and Industrial Societies (1979).

26. See Chapter 1.

27. See Border Security, Economic Opportunity, and Immigration Modernization Act, S. 744, § 2301, 113th Cong., 1st Sess. (2013).

28. See Chapter 9.

29. See Motomura, Americans in Waiting.

CHAPTER 6

1. On Europe, see Philip Connor & Jeffrey S. Passel, Europe's Unauthorized Immigrant Population Peaks in 2016, Then Levels Off (Pew Research Ctr. 2019).

2. See Chapter 3.

3. On this history, see Motomura, Americans in Waiting, at 16–19, 21–26, 125; Motomura, Immigration Outside the Law, at 34–44.

4. On Chinese exclusion, see Act of May 6, 1882, ch. 126, § 14, 22 Stat. 58, 61 (1882); Act of Apr. 27, 1904, ch. 1630, § 5, 33 Stat. 392, 428 (1904); repealed by Act of Dec. 17, 1943, ch. 344, § 1, 57 Stat. 600, 600 (1943). For other restrictions, see Act of Feb. 5, 1917, ch. 29, § 3, 39 Stat. 874, 876. See Act of May 19, 1921, ch. 8, §§ 2(a)(6), 3, 42 Stat. 5, 5–7; Act of May 26, 1924, ch. 190, § 5, 43 Stat. 153, 155. See also Chapter 3.

5. See Immigration Comm'n, Reports of the Immigration Commission: Abstracts of the Reports of the Immigration Commission with Conclusions and Recommendations and Views of the Minority, S. Doc. No. 61,747, at 690–91 (1911).

6. On this era, see Motomura, Immigration Outside the Law, at 31–55.

7. See INA §§ 275, 276, 8 U.S.C. §§ 1325, 1326. On the legislative background, see Brief for Professors Kelly Lytle-Hernandez, Ingrid Eagly, and Mae Ngai.

8. See Chapter 3.

9. See Motomura, Immigration Outside the Law, at 43–45.

10. See Massey, Goldring & Durand, Continuities in Transnational Migration.

11. See Passel & Krogstad, What We Know About Unauthorized Immigrants.

12. See Cecilia Menjívar, The Racialization of "Illegality," 150 (2) Daedalus 91 (2021). On racializing immigrants, see Douglas S. Massey, The Bipartisan Origins of White Nationalism, 150 (2) Daedalus 5 (2021); Zoltan Hajnal, Immigration & the Origins of White Backlash, 150 (2) Daedalus 23 (2021).

13. For discussion of terminology, see Linda Bosniak, Amnesty in Immigration: Forgetting, Forgiving, Freedom, 16 Crit Rev. Int'l Soc. & Pol. Philosophy 344, 344–45 (2013).

14. See Muzaffar Chishti & Charles Kamasaki, IRCA in Retrospect: Guideposts for Today's Immigration Reform (Migration Policy Inst. 2014); Ruth Ellen Wasem, Alien Legalization and Adjustment of Status: A Primer 4 (Cong. Res. Serv. 2010).

15. H.R. 1177, 117th Cong., 1st Sess.

16. Donald M. Kerwin, More than IRCA: U.S. Legalization Programs and the Current Policy Debate 2 (Migration Policy Inst. 2010).

17. See INA § 240A(b), 8 U.S.C. § 1229b(b).

18. See INA § 249, 8 U.S.C. § 1259; INA § 101(a)(27)(J), 8 U.S.C. § 1101(a)(27)(J).

19. See Guillermina Jasso, Douglas S. Massey, Mark R. Rosenzweig & James B. Smith, Illegal to Legal: Estimating Previous Illegal Experience among New Legal Immigrants to the United States, 41 Int'l Migr. Rev. 803 (2008). On legalization, see Michael J. Sullivan, Earned Citizenship (2019); Regine: Regularisations in Europe (Martin Baldwin-Edwards & Albert Kraler eds., 2009); Kevin Fredy Winterberger, Regularisations of Irregularly Staying Migrants in the EU: A Comparative Analysis of Austria, Germany and Spain (2023); Patrick Weil, All or Nothing? What the United States Can Learn From Europe As It Contemplates Circular Migration and Legalization for Undocumented Immigrants (German Marshall Fund of the United States 2010); Sarah Song & Irene Bloemraad, Immigrant Legalization: A Dilemma Between Justice and the Rule of Law, 10 Migr. Stud. 484, 486 (2022); Vusilizwe Thebe, Two Steps Forward, One Step Back: Zimbabwean Migration and South Africa's Regularising Programme (the ZDP), 18 J. Int'l Migr. & Int. 613 (2017); Alan Desmond, Regularization in the European Union and the United States: The Frequent Use of an Exceptional Measure, in 2 Global Migration: Old Assumptions, New Dynamics 69 (Diego Acosta Arcarazo & Anja Wiesbrock eds., 2015); Françoise De Bel-Air, Demography, Migration and Labour Market in Saudi Arabia (Migration Policy Centre 2014); Willem Maas, Unauthorized Migration and the Politics of Regularization, Legalization, and Amnesty, in Labour Migration in Europe 232 (Georg Menz & Alexander Caviedes eds., 2010).

20. See Bosniak, Amnesty in Immigration, at 344, 349–52, 359–61.

21. See S. 365, Dream Act of 2023, 118th Cong., 1st Sess. (DREAM Act); President Barack Obama, Remarks by the President on Immigration (June 15, 2012) (DACA); Memorandum from Janet Napolitano, Sec'y of Homeland Sec., Exercising Prosecutorial Discretion with Respect to Individuals Who Came to The United States as Children (June 15, 2012) (DACA); INA § 101(a)(27)(J), 8 U.S.C. § 101(a)(27)(J) (SIJS); 8 C.F.R. § 204.11 (SIJS).

22. See Hiroshi Motomura, Children and Parents, Innocence and Guilt, 128 Harv. L. Rev. F. 137 (2015). See also Antje Ellermann, The Comparative Politics of Immigration 362–63 (2021) (on how support for legalization may require separating "good" from "bad" undocumented immigrants).

23. See Motomura, Immigration Outside the Law, at 154–65; Sullivan, Earned Citizenship; Shannon Gleeson, Labor Rights for All? The Role of Undocumented Immigrant Status for Worker Claims-Making, 35 L. & Soc. Inq. 561 (2010).

24. See Mollie Gerver, The Case for Permanent Residency for Frontline Workers, 116 Am. Pol. Sci. Rev. 87 (2022).

25. See Andrew Tae-Hyun Kim, Deportation Deadline, 95 Wash. U. L. Rev. 531, 567–69 (2017).

26. See Ricardo D. Martínez-Schuldt & Daniel E. Martínez, Immigrant Sanctuary Policies and Crime-Reporting Behavior: A Multilevel Analysis of Reports of Crime Victimization to Law Enforcement, 1980 to 2004, 86 Am. Soc. Rev. 154–85 (2021).

27. See Chapter 1; Motomura, Americans in Waiting, at 80–95 (immigration as affiliation).

28. On legalization and the rule of law, see Song & Bloemraad, at 486–505. For a different view, see Kris W. Kobach, Reinforcing the Rule of Law: What States Can and Should Do to Reduce Illegal Immigration, 22 Geo. Immigr. L.J. 459 (2008).

29. See Song & Bloemraad, at 493; Catalina Amuedo-Dorantes & Thitima Puttitanun, DACA and the Surge in Unaccompanied Minors at the US–Mexico Border, 54 Int'l Migr. 102, 112 (2016); Tom K. Wong & Hillary Kosnac, Does the Legalization of Undocumented Immigrants in the U.S. Encourage Unauthorized Immigration from Mexico? An Empirical Analysis of the Moral Hazard of Legalization, 55 Int'l Migr. 159, 169 (2017); Frank Wehinger, Do Amnesties Pull in Illegal Immigrants? An Analysis of European Apprehension Data, 1 Int'l J. Migr. & Border Stud. 231 (2014).

30. See Border Security, Economic Opportunity, and Immigration Modernization Act, S. 744, § 2301, 113th Cong., 1st Sess. (2013).

31. See Song & Bloemraad, at 491.

32. On employment, see Motomura, Immigration Outside the Law, at 154–65; Hiroshi Motomura, The Rights of Others: Legal Claims and Immigration Outside the Law, 59 Duke L.J. 1723, 1746–62 (2010). On K–12 public education, see Plyler v. Doe, 457 U.S. 202 (1982). On tax obligations, see Francine J. Lipman, The Taxation of Undocumented Immigrants: Separate, Unequal, and Without Representation, 9 Harv. Latino L. Rev. 1 (2006).

33. See Citizenship for Essential Workers Act, S.1392, 118th Cong., 1st Sess. (2023).

34. See INA § 249, 8 U.S.C. § 1259; Dep't of Homeland Sec., 2021 Yearbook of Immigration Statistics 24, tbl. 7 (2022).

CHAPTER 7

1. See Chapters 4, 5, and 6.

2. See T. Alexander Aleinikoff, David A. Martin, Hiroshi Motomura, Maryellen Fullerton, Juliet Stumpf & Pratheepan Gulasekaram, Immigration and Citizenship: Process and Policy 71–72, 116–17 (9th ed. 2021).

3. See INA § 274A, 8 U.S.C. § 1324a; Immigration and Citizenship: Process and Policy, at 350–53, 952–63.

4. See Illegal Aliens, Ineligibility for Public Services, Verification and Reporting, Proposition 187. On the emergence of the issue in politics, see Motomura, Immigration Outside the Law, at 70–81.

5. See League of United Latin American Citizens v. Wilson, 997 F. Supp. 1244, 1261 (C.D. Cal. 1997); League of United Latin American Citizens v. Wilson, 908 F. Supp. 755 (C.D. Cal. 1995); Motomura, Immigration Outside the Law, at 50.

6. See Illegal Immigration Reform and Immigrant Responsibility Act (IIRIRA), Pub. L. 104–208, 110 Stat. 3009; Motomura, Immigration Outside the Law, at 50; Mark Akkerman, Global Spending on Immigration Enforcement Is Higher than Ever and Rising (Migration Policy Inst. 2023).

7. For further discussion, see Motomura, Immigration Outside the Law, at 56–85.

8. See Immigration and Citizenship: Process and Policy, at 1078–1104; Hiroshi Motomura, Arguing About Sanctuary, 52 U.C. Davis L. Rev. 435, 439–40 (2018).

9. On enforcement discretion, see Motomura, Immigration Outside the Law, at 46–52, 128–30.

10. See Tanya Maria Golash-Boza, Deported: Immigrant Policing, Disposable Labor and Global Capitalism 8 (2015).

11. For an example, see US Dep't of Homeland Sec., Civil Immigration Enforcement: Priorities for the Apprehension, Detention, and Removal of Aliens, Memorandum from Director John Morton for All ICE Employees (March 2, 2011).

12. See Motomura, The President's Dilemma, at 23–26.

13. See Enhancing Public Safety in the Interior of the United States, Exec. Order 13768, 82 Fed. Reg. 8799 (2017).

14. See Chapter 6.

15. See Alexander Tenorio, As a San Diego Neurosurgeon, I See the Devastating Toll of the Raised Border Wall, L.A. Times, Apr. 13, 2023.

16. See Douglas S. Massey, Backfire at the Border: Why Enforcement without Legalization Cannot Stop Illegal Immigration (Cato Inst. 2005).

17. See Douglas S. Massey, The Bipartisan Origins of White Nationalism, 150 (2) Daedalus 5, 5–7 (2021).

18. On lawyers enhancing appearance rates, see Ingrid V. Eagly & Steven Shafer, A National Study of Access to Counsel in Immigration Court, 164 U. Pa. L. Rev. 1, 72–75 (2015).

19. On disengagement and accepting deportation, see Ingrid V. Eagly, Remote Adjudication in Immigration, 109 Nw. U. L. Rev. 933, 977–1000 (2015).

20. See Immigration and Citizenship: Process and Policy, at 843–57; Aguilera-Enriquez v. INS, 516 F.2d 565 (6th Cir. 1975), cert. denied, 423 U.S. 1050 (1976)

21. See Muzaffar Chishti, Doris Meissner, Stephen Yale-Loehr, Kathleen Bush-Joseph & Christopher Levesque, At the Breaking Point: Rethinking the U.S. Immigration Court System (Migration Policy Inst. 2023)

22. See Brooke Williams & Shawn Musgrave, Federal Prosecutors are Using Plea Bargains as a Secret Weapon for Deportations, The Intercept, Nov. 15, 2017.

23. See Chapter 3.

24. Immigration and Citizenship: Process and Policy, at 351.

25. Employer sanctions are in INA § 274A, 8 U.S.C. § 1324a. On the role of transportation companies, see Shachar, The Shifting Border, at 33–35, 81.

26. See Keegan Hamilton, As Border Extremism Goes Mainstream, Vigilante Groups Take a Starring Role, L.A. Times, Dec. 18, 2023.

27. See Arizona v. United States, 567 U.S. 387 (2012).

28. See US DOJ Civil Rights Division, United States Investigation of the Maricopa County Sheriff's Office Findings Letter, Letter Memorandum from Thomas R. Perez, Assistant

US Gen., to Mr. Bill Montgomery, Cnty. Atty. for Maricopa Cnty., Ariz. (Dec. 14, 2011). On limiting discrimination, see Motomura, Immigration Outside the Law, at 135–42.

29. See Chapter 6.

30. See David A. Martin, Resolute Enforcement Is Not Just for Restrictionists: Building a Stable and Efficient Immigration Enforcement System, 30 J.L. & Politics 401, 443–45, 449–54 (2015) (on Obama administration initiatives); Border Security and Immigration Enforcement Improvements, Exec. Order 13767, § 8, 82 Fed. Reg. 8793 (2017) (setting out Trump administration policies); Revision of Civil Immigration Enforcement Policies and Priorities, Exec. Order 13993, 86 Fed. Reg. 7051 (2021) (revoking Trump Exec. Order 13768). On state and local measures, see Motomura, Immigration Outside the Law, at 73–76.

31. See Chapter 3.

32. See INA § 208, 8 U.S.C. § 1158; Sale v. Haitian Centers Council, 509 U.S. 155 (1993).

33. On liability, see Hernandez v. Mesa, 589 U.S. 93 (2020).

34. See Alex Nowrasteh, Enforcement Didn't End Unlawful Immigration in 1950s, More Visas Did, Cato at Liberty Blog, Nov. 11, 2015. See Chapters 4 (admission and exclusion), 6 (legalization), 8 (sharing immigration prosperity), and 9 (addressing root causes of migration).

CHAPTER 8

1. See Chapters 3 and 6.

2. On intertwining of white racial resentment, anti-immigrant attitudes, and partisan polarization, see Douglas S. Massey, The Bipartisan Origins of White Nationalism, 150 (2) Daedalus 5 (2021); Michael Hout & Christopher Maggio, Immigration, Race & Political Polarization, 150 (2) Daedalus 40 (2021); Parker, at 67.

3. See The Economic and Fiscal Consequences of Immigration 1–12 (Francine D. Blau & Christopher Mackie eds., National Academies Press 2017); Law and Economics of Immigration (Howard F. Chang ed. 2015); Giovanni Peri, The Impact of Immigrants in Recession and Economic Expansion (Migration Policy Inst. 2010). On labor market effects, see Kimberly Clausing, Open: The Progressive Case for Free Trade, Immigration, and Global Capital 192–98 (2019).

4. See Peter Coy, What Economists Think About Immigration Doesn't Really Matter, N.Y. Times, Dec. 17, 2021; Economic and Fiscal Consequences, at 266.

5. See Miller, at 10; Song, Immigration and Democracy, at 167; David Abraham, Doing Justice on Two Fronts: The Liberal Dilemma in Immigration, 33 Ethnic & Racial Stud. 968, 976 (2010).

6. See David Card, The Impact of the Mariel Boatlift on the Miami Labor Market, 43 Indus. & Lab. Rel. Rev. 245, 248–50 (1990). For an overview, see Ran Abramitzky & Leah Boustan, Streets of Gold: America's Untold Story of Immigrant Success 139–62 (2022).

7. See Card, Impact of the Mariel Boatlift, at 245, 249; see also David Card, Immigrant Inflows, Native Outflows, and the Local Labor Market Impacts of Higher Immigration, 19 J. Lab. Econ. 22, 57 (2001); Gianmarco I.P. Ottaviano & Giovanni Peri, Rethinking the Gains from Immigration: Theory and Evidence From the U.S. 28 (Nat'l Bureau of Econ. Research 2005).

8. See, e.g., Michael A. Clemens, Economics and Emigration: Trillion Dollar Bills on the Sidewalk?, 25 J. Econ. Persp. 83, 84 (2011); cf. James M. McPherson, Battle Cry of Freedom: The Civil War Era, 1848–1865, at 18 (1988) (on the mid-nineteenth-century labor-saving devices allowing more workers to be engaged in US manufacturing).

9. See Card, Impact of the Mariel Boatlift, at 255–57.

10. On links between immigration and US workers, see Ruth Milkman, History Shows That the Immigrant Threat Narrative Is Wrong, in Immigration Matters: Movements, Visions, and Strategies for a Progressive Future 55, 55–65 (Ruth Milkman, Deepak Bhargava & Penny Lewis eds., 2021). See also Miriam Jordan, As Immigrant Farmworkers Become More Scarce, Robots Replace Humans, N.Y. Times, Nov. 20, 2018; Margaret E. Peters, Trading Barriers: Immigration and the Remaking of Globalization 30 (2017); Arlie Russell Hochschild, Male Trouble, N.Y. Rev. of Books, Oct. 11, 2018 (on "automatability" of occupations).

11. See George J. Borjas, The Economics of Immigration, 32 J. Econ. Lit. 1667, 1674 (1994); George J. Borjas, The Labor Demand Curve is Downward Sloping: Reexamining the Impact of Immigration on the Labor Market, 118 Q. J. Econ. 1335, 1335 (2003); George Borjas, The Immigration Debate We Need, N.Y. Times, Feb. 27, 2017; L. Jason Anastasopoulos, George J. Borjas, Gavin G. Cook & Michael Lachanski, Job Vacancies and Immigration: Evidence from the Mariel Supply Shock, 15 J. Human Capital 1 (2021).

12. See Economic and Fiscal Consequences, at 266.

13. See Francine J. Lipman, Taxing Undocumented Immigrants: Separate, Unequal, and Without Representation, 9 Harv. Latino L. Rev. 1, 4–7 (2006).

14. Compare Jeffrey S. Passel & Rebecca L. Clark, How Much Do Immigrants Really Cost? A Reappraisal of Huddle's "The Cost of Immigrants" (1994), with Borjas, The Economics of Immigration. On empirical challenges, see Economic and Fiscal Consequences, at 202–10.

15. See Economic and Fiscal Consequences, at 7–12. On economic upward mobility for the children and grandchildren of immigrants, see Abramitzky & Boustan, at 73–101.

16. On sharing prosperity, see Clausing, at 228–38.

17. See INA § 214(c)(9), 8 U.S.C. §1184(c)(9); Stuart Anderson, H-1B Visa Fees Create 87,000 College Scholarships for U.S. Students, Forbes, Apr. 4, 2019.

18. See Save America Comprehensive Immigration Act of 2005, H.R. 2092, 109th Cong., 1st Sess. §§ 201, 403 (2005); Border Security, Economic Opportunity, and Immigration Modernization Act, S. 744, 113th Cong., 1st Sess. §§ 4101–05, 4211–14, 4221–25, 4231–37 (2013). On selling or auctioning permits to employers hiring temporary workers, see Alessandra Casella & Adam B. Cox, A Property Rights Approach to Temporary Work Visas, 47 J. Leg. Stud. 195, 204–06 (2018).

19. See Timothy Meyer, Saving the Political Consensus in Favor of Free Trade, 70 Vand. L. Rev. 985, 993–94 (2017).

20. See Katherine Boo, The Churn: Creative Destruction in a Border Town, New Yorker, Mar. 29, 2004, at 62.

21. See Edward Alden, Failure to Adjust: How Americans Got Left Behind in the Global Economy 107–26 (2017); Stephen Kim Park, Bridging the Global Governance Gap: Reforming the Law of Trade Adjustment, 43 Geo. J. Int'l L. 797, 800–01 (2012).

22. See Alden, at 114, 125.

23. See Thomas Friedman, The World Is Flat: A Brief History of the Twenty-First Century 284 (2005); Meyer, at 1017. Another option is identifying and offsetting adverse

effects in advance, which would require more comprehensive industrial policy. See Frank K. Upham, Law and Social Change in Postwar Japan 166–204 (1987).

24. See Economic and Fiscal Consequences, at 207–08 (suggesting program similar to TAA to respond to immigration but acknowledging political obstacles).

25. See Justin Gest, The New Minority: White Working Class Politics in an Age of Immigration and Inequality 2, 63, 157 (2016); Meyer, at 1018; Tyler Cowen, It's Not the Inequality; It's the Immobility, N.Y. Times, Apr. 3, 2015.

26. See Ron Nixon, U.S. Says It Can Pay for 100 Miles of Wall on 2,000-Mile Border, N.Y. Times, Mar. 30, 2018; David J Bier, Why the Wall Won't Work (Cato Inst. 2017).

27. See Jack Miles, Blacks v. Browns, Atl. Monthly (Oct. 1992); see also Carol M. Swain, The Congressional Black Caucus and the Impact of Immigration on African American Unemployment, in Debating Immigration 175 (Carol M. Swain ed., 2007). On post-Katrina New Orleans, see Broken Levees, Broken Promises: New Orleans' Migrant Workers in Their Own Words (Southern Poverty L. Center 2006); Kevin R. Johnson, Hurricane Katrina: Lessons About Immigrants in the Administrative State, 45 Hous. L. Rev. 11, 58–64 (2008).

28. See Hana E. Brown, Jennifer A. Jones & Taylor Dow, Unity in the Struggle: Immigration and the South's Emerging Civil Rights Consensus, 79 L. & Contemp. Probs. 5, 20–23 (2016) (on immigrant advocates' efforts to cast issues as civil rights matters).

29. See John D. Skrentny, Race, Immigration and Civil Rights Law in the Low-Skilled Workplace, in Debating Immigration 21, 25–30 (Carol M. Swain ed., 2007); Jennifer Gordon & R.A. Lenhardt, Rethinking Work and Citizenship, 55 UCLA L. Rev. 1161, 1174–83 (2008).

30. See Christina Tamir, Key Findings about Black Immigrants in the U.S. (Pew Research Center 2022); Bill Ong Hing, Immigration Policies: Messages of Exclusion to African Americans, 37 How. L.J. 237, 259–61 (1994).

31. See Anthony D. Greene, From the Outside In: Black Americans and Black Immigrant's Attitudes Toward Immigrants and Immigration Policy, 25 J. African American Studies 422 (2021); Maureen A. Craig & Jennifer A. Richeson, Hispanic Population Growth Engenders Conservative Shift Among Non-Hispanic Racial Minorities, 9 Soc. Psychol. & Personality Sci. 383, 389–90 (2018); Valerie Russ, Who is Black in America? Ethnic Tensions Flare Between Black Americans and Black Immigrants, Phila. Inquirer, Oct. 19, 2018; Candis Watts Smith, Black Immigrants in the U.S. Face Big Challenges. Will African Americans Rally to Their Side?, Wash. Post, Sept. 18, 2017.

32. See Sarah Smarsh, Liberal Blind Spots Are Hiding the Truth About "Trump Country," N.Y. Times, July 19, 2018 (arguing that race is exaggerated as a factor in resentment).

33. On this history, see Chapter 3; see also Motomura, Immigration Outside the Law, at 41–46.

34. See Irene Browne, Beth Reingold & Anne Kronberg, Race Relations, Black Elites, and Immigration Politics: Conflict, Commonalities, and Context, 96 Soc. Forces 1691, 1696–99, 1714–15 (2018). See also Leann M. Mclaren, Race, Immigration and Black Intergroup Politics, 5 Politics, Groups, & Identities 1, 5 (2024); Helen B. Marrow, Linda R. Tropp, Meta van der Linden & Dina G. Okamoto, How Does Interracial Contact Among the U.S.-Born Shape White and Black Receptivity Toward Immigrants?, 16 Du Bois Rev. 385, 388 (2019); R. Khari Brown, Black Churches and African American Opinion on Immigration Policy, in From Every Mountainside: Black Churches and the Broad Terrain of Civil Rights 315, 323 (R. Drew Smith ed., 2013).

35. See Nat'l Ass'n for the Advancement of Colored People, Creation of a Sustainable Immigration Policy for the United States, Resolution (2023); Nat'l Ass'n for the Advancement of Colored People, Immigration Factsheet and Talking Points 1 (2011); NAACP v. US Dep't Homeland Sec., 364 F. Supp. 3d 568, 572 (D. Md. 2019); cf. Ramos v. Nielsen, 321 F. Supp. 3d 1083, 1098–1105 (N.D. Cal. 2018) (on evidence of Trump's anti-immigrant and anti-Muslim comments).

36. See Kira Gartzou-Katsouyanni, Max Kiefel & José Javier Olivas Osuna, Voting for Your Pocketbook, but against Your Pocketbook? A Study of Brexit at the Local Level, 50 Politics & Society 3 (2021); Danny Hakim, Welsh Reject E.U., but Its Money Will Be Missed, N.Y. Times, July 5, 2016.

37. See Timothy Garton Ash, Only Respect for the "Left Behind" Can Turn the Populist Tide, Guardian, Sept. 28, 2017; Katrin Bennhold, One Legacy of Merkel?: Angry East German Men Fueling the Far Right, N.Y. Times, Nov. 5, 2018; Jan-Werner Müller, Behind the New German Right, N.Y. Rev. Daily, Apr. 14, 2016.

38. See Gest, at 174–78; Jayashri Srikantiah & Shirin Sinnar, White Nationalism as Immigration Policy, 71 Stan. L. Rev. Online 197, 200–02 (2019); Patrick Kingsley, As West Fears the Rise of Autocrats, Hungary Shows What's Possible, N.Y. Times, Feb. 10, 2018; David Leonhardt & Ian Prasad Philbrick, Donald Trump's Racism: The Definitive List, Updated, N.Y. Times, Jan. 15, 2018; Ross Douthat, Between Folly and Cruelty on Immigration, N.Y. Times, July 6, 2019. See also Stuart Chinn, Trump and Chinese Exclusion: Contemporary Parallels With Legislative Debates Over the Chinese Exclusion Act of 1882, 84 Tenn. L. Rev. 681, 687–95 (2017) (distinguishing cultural from racist restrictionism). On enforcement's role in warding off such arguments, see Martin, Resolute Enforcement.

39. See US Cit. & Immigr. Servs., USCIS Director L. Francis Cissna on New Agency Mission Statement (Feb. 22, 2018).

40. See Steven Greenhouse, The Unions that Like Trump, N.Y. Times, Apr. 8, 2017; Anna Maria Mayda, Who Is Against Immigration? A Cross-Country Investigation of Individual Attitudes Toward Immigrants 25–27 (IZA Inst. of Labor & Econ. 2004); Kenneth F. Scheve & Matthew J. Slaughter, Labor Market Competition and Individual Preferences over Immigration Policy, 83 Rev. Econ. & Stats. 133, 143–44 (2001).

CHAPTER 9

1. See Chapters 5, 6, and 7.

2. See Peters, at 30 (on cross-border free trade reducing private sector support for admitting workers that have less education or skill).

3. See Peter Baker, Trump Signs New Trade Deal with Canada and Mexico After Bitter Negotiations, N.Y. Times, Nov. 30, 2018; Dolores Acevedo & Thomas J. Espenshade, Implications of a North American Free Trade Agreement for Mexican Migration into the United States, 18 Population & Dev. Rev. 729, 731 (1992); Patricia Fernández-Kelly & Douglas S. Massey, Borders for Whom? The Role of NAFTA in Mexico–U.S. Migration, 610 Annals Am. Acad. Pol. & Soc. Sci. 98, 105 (2007); Gordon & Lenhardt, at 1114; Jeff Faux, How NAFTA Failed Mexico: Immigration Is Not a Development Policy, Am. Prospect, July–Aug. 2003, at 35.

4. See Chapter 5 (on temporary versus indefinite). See also Demetrios G. Papademetriou, Gunter Sugiyarto, Dovelyn Rannveig Mendoza & Brian Salant, Achieving Skill Mobility in the ASEAN Economy Community 20–21 (Migration Policy Inst. 2015); Jennifer Gordon, People Are Not Bananas: How Immigration Differs from Trade, 104 Nw. U. L. Rev. 1109, 1119–21 (2010).

5. See James F. Hollifield, Governing Migration: Public Goods and Private Partnerships, in Free Movement of Workers and Labour Market Adjustment, at 277, 282 (OECD 2012).

6. On trade and individual rights, see James F. Hollifield, Immigrants, Markets, and States: The Political Economy of Postwar Europe 131, 230–31 (1992); James F. Hollifield, The Emerging Migration State, 38 Int'l Migr. Rev. 885, 900–05 (2004). On NAFTA's effects, see Juan Gonzalez, Harvest of Empire: A History of Latinos in the United States 265–71 (rev. ed. 2011).

7. The Refugee Convention lacks any responsibility-sharing structure, which would have undercut the premise of national sovereignty. See Aleinikoff & Zamore, at 13. The New York Declaration for Refugees and Migrants, adopted by the U.N. General Assembly in 2016, addresses shared responsibility. See G.A. Res. 71/1. In 2024, the European Union adopted a burden-sharing scheme among EU countries based on each country's GDP and population.

8. On the option to stay or return, see 2018 United Nations' Global Compact for Safe, Orderly and Regular Migration (calling for addressing migration at its source). G.A. Res. 73/195. The United States withdrew from the Compact in 2017. See Megan Specia, U.N. Agrees on Migration Pact, but U.S. Is Conspicuously Absent, N.Y. Times, July 13, 2018.

9. See Michael A. Clemens & Hannah M. Postel, Deterring Emigration with Foreign Aid: An Overview of Evidence from Low-Income Countries, 44 Population & Dev. Rev. 667, 675–78, 683 (2018); see also Wilbur Zelinsky, The Hypothesis of the Mobility Transition, 61 Geo. Rev. 219 (1971); Heaven Crawley & Brad K. Blitz, Common Agenda or Europe's Agenda? International Protection, Human Rights and Migration from the Horn of Africa, 45 J. Ethnic & Migr. Stud. 2258, 2261 (2019); Loren B. Landau, Caroline Wanjiku Kihato & Hannah Postel, Europe Is Making Its Migration Problem Worse: The Dangers of Aiding Autocrats, Foreign Aff., Sept. 5, 2018; Hein De Haas, Migration and Development: A Theoretical Perspective, 44 Int'l Migr. Rev. 227, 228 (2010); Jean-Claude Berthélemy, Monica Beuran & Mathilde Maurel, Aid and Migration: Substitutes or Complements?, 37 World Dev. 1589, 1589 (2009).

10. See Mauro Lanati & Rainer Thiele, The Impact of Foreign Aid on Migration Revisited, 111 World Dev. 59, 60 (2018). On youth employment, see Nicholas Kristof, This Teenager Knows a Secret to Slowing Guatemalan Migration, N.Y. Times, June 8, 2019; Clemens & Postel, at 680–83.

11. On aid in rural areas, see Jonas Gamso & Farhod Yuldashev, Targeted Foreign Aid and International Migration: Is Development-Promotion an Effective Immigration Policy?, 62 Int'l Stud. Q. 809, 809 (2018); Jonas Gamso & Farhod Yuldashev, Does Rural Development Aid Reduce International Migration?, 110 World Dev. 268, 273, 277 (2018); Douglas S. Massey, Economic Development and International Migration in Comparative Perspective, 14 Population & Dev. Rev. 383, 388–90 (1988).

12. See Gamso & Yuldashev, Rural Development, at 269.

13. On prosperity over time and links between development and migration, see Michael A. Clemens, The Emigration Life Cycle: How Development Shapes Emigration from Poor

Countries, (Inst. of Labor Economics Aug. 2020); Susan Fratzke & Brian Salant, Moving Beyond "Root Causes": The Complicated Relationship between Development and Migration (Migration Policy Inst. 2018).

14. See Muzaffar Chishti & Doris Meissner, America's Border Dilemma: Why Biden Has Few Good Options on Immigration, Foreign Affairs, Nov. 23, 2021; Andrew Selee, On Migration, Will the Americas Succeed Where Europe Could Not?, N.Y. Times, Oct. 27, 2021. On violence and migration, see Sonia Nazario, How to Secure the Border: Spoiler Alert: A Wall Won't Do It, Opinion, L.A. Times, Apr. 23, 2017; Crawley & Blitz, at 2270–71.

15. On Mexican management of migration from Central America, see Laurent Faret, María Eugenia Anguiano Téllez & Luz Helena Rodríguez-Tapia, Migration Management and Changes in Mobility Patterns in the North and Central American Region, J. Migr. & Human Sec. (2021). On migration from China to and through Mexico, see Eileen Sullivan, Growing Numbers of Chinese Migrants Are Crossing the Southern Border, N.Y. Times, Nov. 24, 2023. On the decline in the Mexican share of the US unauthorized population, see Warren, at 283–84.

16. See Decision No 1/2016 of the EU-Jordan Association Committee of July 19, 2016, 2016 O.J. (L 233) 6; European Commission, Report on EU-Jordan Relations in the Framework of the Revised ENP (June 13, 2017); Alexander Betts & Paul Collier, Refuge: Rethinking Refugee Policy in a Changing World 168–76 (2017) (on the Jordan Compact); Marion Panizzon, The EU-Jordan Compact in a Trade Law Context: Preferential Access to the EU Market to "Keep Refugees in the Region," in Constitutionalising the External Dimensions of EU Migration Policies in Times of Crisis: Legality, Rule of Law and Fundamental Rights Reconsidered 220 (Sergio Carrera, Juan Santos Vara & Tineke Strik eds., 2019).

17. See Chapter 2. See also Veronique Barbelet, Jessica Hagen-Zanker & Dina Mansour-Ille, The Jordan Compact: Lessons Learnt and Implications for Future Refugee Compacts 3–6 (2018) (on the EU-Jordan Compact); Heliodoro Temprano Arroyo, Encouraging the Employment of Refugees Through Trade Preferences 4–5 (Migration Policy Ctr. 2017) (same).

18. See Barbelet, Hagen-Zanker & Mansour-Ille; Izza Leghtas, Out of Reach: Legal Work Still Inaccessible to Refugees in Jordan 15 (Overseas Dev. Inst. 2018); Vicky Kelberer & Denis Sullivan, Challenges and Successes of Jordan's Work Permit Program for Syrian Refugees After One Year, Atl. Council, Mar. 27, 2017; Temprano Arroyo, at 1, 3.

19. See Jennifer Gordon, Investing in Low-Wage Jobs Is the Wrong Way to Reduce Migration, Foreign Pol'y, Jan. 28, 2019.

20. See European Council Press Release 870/15, Meeting of Heads of State or Government with Turkey, EU-Turkey Statement (Nov. 29, 2015). As of 2018, over 3.5 million Syrian migrants were registered officially in Turkey. See United Nations High Comm'r for Refugees, Turkey, Turkey Protection Sector Q3, July–Sept. 2018 (2018).

21. On Mexico, see Azam Ahmed & Kirk Semple, Mexico Mulls Allowing Migrants to Stay There Pending U.S. Asylum Bids, N.Y. Times, Nov. 24, 2018; Amy Guthrie, Incoming Mexico Gov't: No Deal to Host US Asylum-Seekers, Assoc. Press, Nov. 25, 2018.

22. See, e.g., Daniel Trilling, Should We Build a Wall Around North Wales?, 39 London Rev. Books 15, 15–18 (2017); Christopher Bertram, Reforming Refuge, New Humanist,

Aug. 29, 2017; Ian Birrell, Refuge: Transforming a Broken Refugee System Review—Flawed and Frustrating, Guardian, July 30, 2017; Gordon, Investing in Low-Wage Jobs.

23. See Abby Sewell, EU Announced 1 Billion Euros in Aid for Lebanon Amid a Surge in Irregular Migration, AP News, May 2, 2024; Nosmat Gbadamosi, How Tunisia Became Europe's Border Guard, Foreign Policy, Sept. 20, 2023; Lutz Oette & Mohamed Abdel-salam Babiker, Migration Control à la Khartoum: EU External Engagement and Human Rights Protection in the Horn of Africa, 36 Refugee Surv. Q. 64, 65, 74 (2017). In 2015, the EU committed 3.2 billion Euros to its Emergency Trust Fund for Africa. The price includes cooperation with the EU on migration control. See European Comm'n, EU Emergency Trust Fund for Africa 1 (Nov. 24, 2017). See also Rebecca Rosman, Africa: Will EU-Africa Deal Depend on Curbing Migration?, All Africa, June 9, 2016; Kristy Siegfried, Five False Assumptions Driving EU Migration Policy, New Humanitarian, June 2, 2015.

24. See Implementing Bilateral and Multilateral Asylum Cooperative Agreements Under the Immigration and Nationality Act, 84 Fed. Reg. 63994 (2019). On externalization, see Shachar, The Shifting Border; Gerda Heck & Sabine Hess, Tracing the Effects of the EU-Turkey Deal, 3 Movements 35, 38–40 (2017); Thomas Gammeltoft-Hansen & James C. Hathaway, Non-Refoulement in a World of Cooperative Deterrence, 53 Colum. J. Transnat'l L. 235, 235 (2015). For criticism of the EU-Turkey Agreement, see Annelies Zoomers, Femke van Noorloos & Ilse van Liempt, Will Tailor-Made Migration Deals Help to Solve the European Migration Crisis?, in The Migration Crisis?, at 105 (2018).

25. See, e.g., Narin Idriz, The EU-Turkey Statement or the 'Refugee Deal': The Extra-Legal Deal of Extraordinary Times?, in The Migration Crisis?, at 61, 62 (2018); Patrick Kingsley, By Stifling Migration, Sudan's Feared Secret Police Aid Europe, N.Y. Times, Apr. 22, 2018. On heightening oppression and human rights violations, see Rep. of the Special Rapporteur on the Human Rights of Migrants, ¶ 73, U.N. Doc. A/68/283 (2013).

26. See Loren B. Landau, A Chronotope of Containment Development: Europe's Migrant Crisis and Africa's Reterritorialisation, 51 Antipode 169, 172–73 (2019); Kate Hooper & Kathleen Newland, Mind the Gap: Bringing Migration into Development Partnerships and Vice Versa 6 (Migration Policy Inst. & German Dev. Coop. Agency 2018); Kevin Sieff, U.S. Officials Said Aid to El Salvador Helped Slow Migration. Now Trump Is Canceling It., Wash. Post, Apr. 1, 2019.

27. See Judt, at 89–99; Curt Tarnoff, The Marshall Plan: Design, Accomplishments, and Significance (Cong. Res. Serv. 2018) (citing numerous sources); Bret Stephens, An Immigration Policy Worse Than Trump's, N.Y. Times, July 5, 2019 (urging "nation building" as a response to migration).

28. See Crawley & Blitz (on security and protection of basic rights more than poverty as drivers of emigration).

29. See Francisco Alba, Mexico at a Crossroads Once More: Emigration Levels Off as Transit Migration and Immigration Rise (Migration Policy Inst. 2024); Raquel Rosenbloom & Jeanne Batalova, Mexican Immigrants in the United States (Migration Policy Inst. 2022); Damien Cave, In Mexican Villages, Few Are Left to Dream of U.S., N.Y. Times, Apr. 2, 2013; Joshua Chaffin, Young Poles Leave UK to Return Home as Economy Booms, Financial Times, Oct. 27, 2017.

30. See Steven Erlanger & Katrin Bennhold, E.U. Reaches Deal on Migration at Summit, but Details Sketchy, N.Y. Times, June 28, 2018. On this phase of EU expansion, see Judt, at 713–36; Rachel A. Epstein, Eastern Enlargement Ten Years On: Transcending the East-West Divide?, 52 J. Common Market Studies 1 (2013); Jacek Wiekclawski, The Eastern Enlargement of the European Union: Fears, Challenges, and Reality, 15 Globality Studies J. 1 (2010).

31. See Douglas S. Massey, Jorge Durand & Nolan J. Malone, Beyond Smoke and Mirrors: Mexican Migration in an Era of Economic Integration 161 (2002); Guy Stecklov, Paul Winters, Marco Stampini & Benjamin Davis, Do Conditional Cash Transfers Influence Migration? A Study Using Experimental Data from the Mexican PROGRESA Program, 42 Demography 769, 787 (2005).

32. See Zoomers, van Noorloos & van Liempt, at 112–15. On remittances as returns on migration as an investment, see Michael A. Clemens & Timothy N. Ogden, Migration and Household Finances: How a Different Framing Can Improve Thinking About Migration, 38 Dev. Policy Rev. 3 (2020). See also G.A. Res. 73/195, ¶ 16; Hooper & Newland, at 6. Total worldwide remittances to low- and middle-income countries in 2023 were an estimated $669 billion. See Leveraging Diaspora Finances for Private Capital Mobilization (World Bank Group 2023).

33. See SeyedSoroosh Azizi, The Impact of Workers' Remittances on Poverty and Inequality in Developing Countries, 60 Empirical Economics 969 (2019); Pablo Acosta, Cesar Calderón, Pablo Fajnzylber & Humberto Lopez, What is the Impact of International Remittances on Poverty and Inequality in Latin America?, 36 World Dev. 89 (2008); German Federal Chancellor Angela Merkel, Office of the German Federal Chancellor, Statement to the European Parliament in Strasbourg (Oct. 7, 2015).

34. See Md. Rubel Islam & Kang-Kook Lee, Do Foreign Remittances Promote Democracy? A Dynamic Panel Study of Developing Countries, 64 Hitotsubashi J. Econ. 59 (2023); Abel Escribà-Folch, Covadonga Meseguer & Joseph Wright, Remittances and Democratization, 59 Int'l Studies Q. 571 (2015). For a cautious assessment of remittances as a vehicle for economic development, Hein de Haas & Simona Vezzoli, Time to Temper the Faith: Comparing the Migration and Development Experiences of Mexico and Morocco (Migration Policy Inst. 2010).

35. See Fitzgerald, Nation of Emigrants, at 55–69, 110–24 (on hometown associations as a corrective for local and regional governments); Song, Immigration and Democracy, at 90 (on remittances going to "the more privileged").

36. See Chapter 5.

37. See U.N. High Commissioner for Refugees, Global Trends: Forced Displacement in 2023, at 21 (2024); Jacqueline Bhabha, Can We Solve the Migration Crisis? 64 (2018). See Betts & Collier, at 179–81; Katy Long & Sarah Rosengaertner, Protection Through Mobility: Opening Labor and Study Migration Channels to Refugees 8 (Migration Policy Inst. 2016).

38. See Jennifer Gordon, The International Governance of Refugee Work: Reflections on the Jordan Compact, 1 Glob. Pub. Pol'y & Governance 239, 244–49 (2021).

39. See Barbelet, Hagen-Zanker & Mansour-Ille, at 53–54; Zoomers, van Noorloos & van Liempt, at 112; Oette & Babiker, at 72; Jennifer Rankin, $2bn EU-Africa 'Anti-Migration' Fund Too Opaque, Say Critics, Guardian, Oct. 31, 2017; Jonathan Slagter,

An "Informal" Turn in the European Union's Migrant Returns Policy Towards Sub-Saharan Africa (Migration Policy Inst. 2019). On resulting labor exploitation, retrenchment of economic and political power in developing countries, and neocolonialism, see Aleinikoff & Zamore, at 25; B. S. Chimni, The Geopolitics of Refugee Studies: View from the South, 11 J. Ref. Stud., 350, 361 (1998).

40. See Landau, Kihato & Postel, Europe Is Making Its Migration Problem Worse (on the EU Trust Fund for Africa as almost entirely outside European Parliament oversight). Traders, investors, and some employees are admitted on exceptionally favorable terms as E-1 and E-2 nonimmigrants if their country has a treaty with the United States. See INA § 101(a)(15)(E), 8 U.S.C. § 1101(a)(15)(E) (2012). Citizens of Chile and Singapore have favorable terms for temporary admission to the United States under trade agreements. See INA § 214(g)(8)(A), 8 U.S.C. § 1184(g)(8)(A) (2012); US-Chile Free Trade Agreement, US-Chile, ch. 14, § 3, June 6, 2003; US-Singapore Free Trade Agreement, US-Sing. ch. 11, § 3, May 6, 2003.

CHAPTER 10

1. See Chapter 1.
2. On the mid-1800s, see John Higham, Strangers in the Land: Patterns of American Nativism, 1860–1925, at 77–87 (rev. ed. 2002); Peter Schrag, Not Fit for Our Society: Immigration and Nativism in America (2010). On post-9/11 developments, see Leti Volpp, The Citizen and The Terrorist, 49 UCLA L. Rev. 1575 (2002); Proclamation No. 9645, Enhancing Vetting Capabilities and Processes for Detecting Attempted Entry Into the United States by Terrorists or Other Public-Safety Threats, 82 Fed. Reg. 45161 (2017).
3. Important exceptions are Angela R. Riley & Kristen A. Carpenter, Decolonizing Indigenous Migration, 109 Calif. Law Rev. 63 (2021); Leti Volpp, The Indigenous as Alien, 5 U.C. Irvine L. Rev. 289 (2015).
4. See Alexander Bickel, The Morality of Consent 53 (1975). On citizenship for Native Americans, see Elk v. Wilkins, 112 U.S. 94 (1884); Allotment Act, U.S. Pub. L. 49–105, 24 Stat. 388 (1887); Indian Citizenship Act, U.S. Pub. L. 68–175, 43 Stat. 253 (1924).
5. See Janet M. Calvo, Spouse-Based Immigration Laws: The Legacies of Coverture, 28 San Diego L. Rev. 593 (1991); Leti Volpp, Divesting Citizenship: On Asian American History and the Loss of Citizenship, 53 UCLA L. Rev. 405 (2005).
6. See Ingrid V. Eagly, Remote Adjudication in Immigration, 109 Nw. U. L. Rev. 933 (2015).
7. Denial of Justice: The Biden Administration's Dedicated Docket in the Boston Immigration Court (Harvard Immigr. & Refugee Clinical Program 2023); The Biden Administration's Dedicated Docket: Inside Los Angeles' Accelerated Court Hearings for Families Seeking Asylum (UCLA Immigrants' Rights Policy Clinic 2022); Sarah Pierce, As the Trump Administration Seeks to Remove Families, Due-Process Questions over Rocket Dockets Abound (Migration Policy Inst. 2019).
8. See Chapters 6 and 7; Motomura, Immigration Outside the Law, at 128–30.
9. See Executive Order 13768, Enhancing Public Safety in the Interior of the United States, 82 Fed. Reg. 8799 (2017), revoked by Revision of Civil Immigration Enforcement Policies and Priorities, 86 Fed. Reg. 7051 (2021). For pre-Trump guidelines, see Memorandum from Secretary of Homeland Sec. Jeh Johnson, Civil Immigration

Enforcement: Priorities for the Apprehension, Detention, and Removal of Undocumented Immigrants (Nov. 20, 2014); Memorandum from Director of Homeland Sec. John Morton, Civil Immigration Enforcement: Priorities for the Apprehension, Detention, and Removal of Aliens (Mar. 20, 2011); Memorandum from Assistant Secretary of Homeland Sec. John Morton, Civil Immigration Enforcement: Priorities for the Apprehension, Detention, and Removal of Aliens (June 30, 2010).

10. See Motomura, The President's Dilemma, at 22–28. See also Michael Kagan, Binding the Enforcers: The Administrative Law Struggle Behind President Obama's Immigration Actions, 50 U. Rich. L. Rev. 665, 684–89 (2016); Adam B. Cox & Cristina M. Rodríguez, The President and Immigration Law Redux, 125 Yale L.J. 104, 135–42 (2015); Anil Kalhan, Deferred Action, Supervised Enforcement Discretion, and the Rule of Law Basis for Executive Action on Immigration, 63 UCLA L. Rev. Disc. 58, 77–78 (2015); Ahilan Arulanantham, The President's Relief Program as a Response to Insurrection, Balkinization, Nov. 25, 2014.

11. See INA §§ 236(a), 240A, 8 U.S.C. §§ 1226, 1229b.

12. See Chapter 7.

13. See Chapter 7; Arizona v. United States, 567 U.S. 387 (2012); Hiroshi Motomura, Federalism, International Human Rights, and Immigration Exceptionalism, 70 U. Colo. L. Rev. 1361–94 (1999).

14. See Chapter 7; see also Motomura, Immigration Outside the Law, at 142–43.

15. See Motomura, Arguing About Sanctuary; Pratheepan Gulasekaram, Rick Su & Rose Cuison Villazor, Anti-Sanctuary and Immigration Localism, 119 Colum. L. Rev. 837 (2019): Christopher N. Lasch, R. L. Chan, Ingrid V. Eagly, Dina F. Haynes, Annie Lai, Elizabeth M. McCormick & Juliet P. Stumpf, Understanding "Sanctuary Cities", 59 Boston Coll. L. Rev. 1703 (2018): Michael Kagan, What We Talk About When We Talk About Sanctuary Cities, 52 U.C. Davis L. Rev. 392 (2018).

16. See Motomura, Immigration Outside the Law, at 151–54. For criticism, David S. Rubenstein, Black-Box Immigration Federalism, 114 Mich. L. Rev. 983 (2016).

17. See John Ruwitch, U.S. Evacuations in Afghanistan Evoke Memories of Saigon's Fall, National Public Radio, Aug. 20, 2021; Marvin Ott, Afghanistan: Echoes of Vietnam? (Wilson Center 2019); Julia Gelatt & Doris Meissner, Straight Path to Legal Permanent Residence for Afghan Evacuees Would Build on Strong U.S. Precedent (Migration Policy Inst. 2022); US Dep't of Homeland Sec., DHS Announces Upcoming Re-parole Process for Afghan Nationals (May 5, 2023).

18. See Chapter 6.

19. See INA §§ 275, 276, 8 U.S.C. §§ 1325, 1326; Brief for Professors Kelly Lytle-Hernandez, Ingrid Eagly, and Mae Ngai. See also Chapter 6.

20. See United States v. Carrillo-Lopez, 555 F. Supp. 3d 996 (D. Nev. 2021), rev'd, 68 F.4th 1133 (9th Cir. 2023).

21. See Village of Arlington Heights v. Metropolitan Housing Development Corp., 429 U.S. 252 (1977); Ahilan Arulanantham, Reversing Racist Precedent, 112 Geo. L.J. 439 (2024).

22. See Chapter 3.

23. See Sylvia Goodman, Researchers Did a Deep Dive Into Efforts to Restrict Critical Race Theory. Here's What They Found, Chron. Higher Educ., Aug. 3, 2022.

24. On the Treaty of Guadalupe Hidalgo, see Laura Gomez, Inventing Latinos: A New Story of American Racism (2020); McPherson, at 3–5.

25. See Chapter 3.

26. See Peter Baker, Trump Signs New Trade Deal with Canada and Mexico After Bitter Negotiations, N.Y. Times, Nov. 30, 2018.

27. Judt, at 829.

28. On reaching back to the past, see Miller, at 77, 113–14; Song, Immigration and Democracy, at 81–84, 115; E. Tendayi Achiume, Migration as Decolonization, 71 Stan. L. Rev. 1509 (2019); Linda Bosniak, Wrongs, Rights and Regularization, 3 Moral Phil. & Pol. 187, 210 (2016); Rogers M. Smith, Living in a Promiseland? Mexican Immigration and American Obligations, 9 Persp. on Politics 545, 545 (2011); cf. Suketu Mehta, Why Should Immigrants "Respect Our Borders"? The West Never Respected Theirs, N.Y. Times, June 7, 2019.

29. On US intervention in Latin America, see Greg Grandin, Empire's Workshop: Latin America, the United States, and the Rise of the New Imperialism (rev. ed. 2021).

30. See Ariela Gross, The Constitution of History and Memory, in Law and the Humanities: An Introduction 416 (Austin Sarat, Matthew Anderson & Cathrine O. Frank eds., 2009).

Index

For the benefit of digital users, indexed terms that span two pages (e.g., 52–53) may, on occasion, appear on only one of those pages.

A

Abbott, Greg, 54
accountability, 107–108, 113, 114, 116, 140–141, 145–146, 149, 153–155
addressing migration's root causes
  accountability and, 145–146
  Bracero program and, 134
  countries of origin and, 136–137
  economic development and, 136–137, 140, 141–145
  EU-Jordan Compact on Immigration (2016) and, 138
  EU policies and, 139, 142, 145–146
  finding ways forward and, 141–143
  international cooperation and, 134–135
  labor migration and, 134–135
  lawful migration pathways and, 142–143, 145
  making immigration policy alone and, 134–135
  Marshall Plan and, 141–142
  North American Free Trade Agreement (NAFTA) and, 134–135
  outsourcing of border control and, 139–141
  overview of, 133–134
  remittances and, 143–145
  transit countries and, 137–141
  transparency and, 145–146
  United States-Mexico-Canada Trade Agreement and, 134
  urban and rural development aid and, 136–137
  US immigration from Mexico and, 137–138
adopted children, 57, 60
advocacy efforts, 41, 46, 49, 93, 130

African Americans and migration, 41, 46, 87, 121, 127–130
agreements with transit countries, 21, 29–30, 135, 137–141
Anglo-Saxon racial superiority claims, 43–45, 88, 112, 157
annual diversity lottery, 67, 128
application process for asylum, 26, 30, 31
Arizona Senate Bill 1070, 113–114
Asiatic barred zone, 44
asylum. *See* forced migration
author experience of borders and belonging, 1–2, 5–7, 162–163

B

belonging claims
  civil rights framework and, 47–50, 53–54
  definition of, 20
  discretion and, 152–153
  discrimination and, 20–22
  enforcement and, 104–105, 108, 114, 116
  getting in and keeping out and, 58–60, 64–67
  humanity claims and, 9–11
  immigration policy and, 21
  insiders and, 20–21
  integration and, 21–22
  land laws and, 21–22
  national borders and, 20–22
  overview of, 9–11, 152–155
  people without lawful status and, 90, 94
  racial restrictions on US citizenship and, 22
  temporary and indefinite stays and, 81
Berra, Yogi, 8–9

better responses to forced migration
  alternatives to asylum and, 32–37
  broadening definition of refugee
    and, 32–37
  definition of forced migrants and, 23–24
  discretion and, 25–27, 31
  discrimination and, 38–40
  distinguishing refugees from other
    migrants and, 32–37
  humanity claims and, 36–39
  immigration policy that considers all
    migrants, 38
  managing and limiting protection
    and, 28–31
  narrowness of protection condition
    and, 32–33
  overview of, 23–24, 37–40
  protecting under stress and, 27–28
  protection approaches and, 32–36
  recommendations for, 37–40
  refugee protection since WW II
    and, 24–27
  shortcomings of alternatives to asylum
    and, 36
  subsidiary protection and, 34
  US immigration from Mexico
    and, 28–31
  work-based admissions and, 38
Bickel, Alexander, 150
Biden, Joe
  applications for refugee status and, 31
  border closure under, 31
  parole and, 36, 39, 59–60, 72–75
  refugee admissions and, 26
  Trump border policies continued
    under, 30–31
birthright citizenship, 42
borders and belonging. See also belonging
    claims
  Achilles heel of a fair and just society
    and, 18, 147–148
  audience of current volume on, 6–7
  author experience of, 1–2, 5–7,
    162–163
  belonging claims and, 9–11, 152–155
  colonialism and, 150
  DACA and, 153
  definition of, 2
  delegation and, 154–155

  disclaimers about, 5–7
  discretion and, 152–155
  discrimination and, 149–150, 152–159
  disruptive ideas about, 4–5
  economic class and, 150
  effects of immigration on long-time
    citizens and, 4–5
  enforcement and, 155
  fair and accurate results and, 151–152
  gender and, 150
  goals of immigration policy, 159–160
  history's role in immigration policy
    and, 4–5, 156–159
  humanity claims and, 9–11, 148–149,
    152–156
  human rights and, 4
  immigration policy and, 3, 151–156
  injustices concealed by border and, 3,
    147–151
  key themes on, 3–4
  methodological approaches and, 8–11
  motivation for current
    volume on, 162–163
  moving forward on, 162–163
  Muslim ban and, 149–150
  open borders concern and, 5
  oversimplification of distinctions
    between types migrants and, 4
  overview of, 1–3, 147
  realistic and utopian approaches
    and, 8–11, 159–160
  realistic utopia approach and, 9–11
  religion and, 149
  structure of current volume on, 7–8
  time as crucial dimension in responses to
    immigration and, 4
  TPS and, 153
  undocumented immigration
    and, 156–159
  use of "crisis" to describe immigration
    and, 2–3
  US immigration from Mexico
    and, 158–159
  US policies and, 151
Borjas, George, 122
Bracero program, 47–48, 88, 89, 134
Brown v. Board of Education (1954), 48

C
Card, David, 121
Cartagena Declaration on Refugees
    (1984), 33
CAT (Convention Against Torture), 26
causes of migration. See addressing
    migration's root causes
child separation, 30
Chinese exclusion, 43, 46
citizenship, 22, 42–43, 150
Civil Rights Act (1964), 46
civil rights framework
    advocacy efforts and, 49
    Anglo-Saxon racial superiority claims
        and, 43–44
    Asiatic barred zone and, 44
    belonging claims and, 47–50, 53–54
    birthright citizenship and, 42
    Bracero program and, 47–48
    Chinese exclusion and, 43, 46
    Civil Rights Act and, 46
    Civil War and, 42–43
    DACA and, 50
    defining insiders and, 50–51
    definition of, 41–42
    demographic change and, 46
    development of, 46–50
    discrimination and, 42–48
    eugenics and, 44–45
    Fourteenth Amendment and, 42
    Gentlemen's Agreement (Japan) and, 44
    Homestead Act and, 43–44
    Immigration Act (1965) and, 46
    interests of insiders and, 52–53
    lawful permanent resident status
        and, 46–47, 50
    limits of national belonging and, 53–54
    limits on immigration numbers and, 44
    national security concerns and, 52
    overview of, 41–42
    race in immigration history and, 42–45
    slavery and, 42
    Supreme Court (US) and, 42, 46–50,
        52–53
    Temporary Protected Status (TPS)
        and, 50
    turning to civil rights and, 46–50
    Undesirable Aliens Act (1929) and, 45

undocumented immigration
    and, 47–49, 51
    US immigration from Mexico and, 45
    Voting Rights Act and, 46
Civil War (US), 42–43
Clemens, Michael, 136
Clinton, Bill, 103
Convention Against Torture (CAT), 26
countries of origin. See addressing
    migration's root causes
COVID-19, 30, 62
"crises" in immigration, 2–3
Cuban immigrants, 72, 121
cultural anxiety, 131

D
Dayton Accords (1995), 38
deeper anxieties, 130–132
Deferred Action for Childhood Arrivals
    (DACA)
    borders and belonging and, 153
    civil rights framework and, 50
    definition of, 50
    enforcement and, 107
    people without lawful status and, 93,
        96–97
    temporary and indefinite stays and, 71,
        73–75, 77
definition of refugee and asylum status. See
    better responses to forced migration;
    forced migration; getting in and
    keeping out; protection approaches
Department of State v. Muñoz
    (2024), 52–53
Dillingham Commission (1907), 87
Din, Fauzia, 52
Din, Kerry v. (2015), 52
discretion
    better responses to forced migration
        and, 25–27, 31
    borders and belonging and, 152–155
    enforcement and, 104–108
    humanity claims and, 152–153
    immigration policy and, 152–155
    people without lawful status and, 88–90
discrimination
    belonging claims and, 20–22
    better responses to forced migration
        and, 38–40

discrimination (*Continued*)
  borders and belonging and, 149–150,
    152–159
  civil rights framework and, 42–48
  enforcement and, 106–108, 112
  getting in and keeping out and, 65–67
  labor and race and, 86–90
  race in immigration history and, 42–45
  taking skeptics seriously and, 127–130
Doe, Plyler v. (1982), 48–49
DREAM (Development, Relief, and
    Education for Alien Minors) Act, 93
Dred Scott v. Sandford (1857), 42

E

E-1 and E-2 categories, 71
economic anxiety, 124–127
economic development, 77–78, 136–137,
    140, 141–145
economic effects of migration, 120–123
economic migration, 62–64, 85, 134–135
Einstein, Albert, 8–9
Eisenhower, Dwight D., 72
enforcement
  approaches to, 108–115
  Arizona Senate Bill 1070 and, 113–114
  belonging claims and, 104–105, 108,
    114, 116
  border enforcement, 30
  child separation and, 30
  criminal penalties and, 111–112
  DACA and, 107
  databases and, 114–115
  detention for, 110
  DHS and, 107
  discretion and, 104–108
  discrimination and, 106–108, 112
  enforcement outside physical borders
    and, 115
  family separation and, 30
  humanity claims and, 19, 104, 108–109,
    114, 116
  Immigration and Customs Enforcement
    (ICE) and, 107
  inadequate process for, 110–111
  intensifying of, 102–104
  overview of, 101–102
  privatized enforcement and, 112–113
  Proposition 187 and, 103
  reform and its limits and, 115–116
  state and local enforcement
    and, 113–114
  transparency and, 107–108
  USCIS and, 107
  US immigration from Mexico and, 103,
    109, 112
  US policies and, 102–104, 107, 114–115
  walls for, 109
ethnicity. *See* discrimination
eugenics, 44–45
EU-Horn of Africa Migration Route
    Initiative (2014), 139
European Union (EU) policies
  addressing migration's root causes
    and, 139, 142, 145–146
  agreements with transit countries
    and, 29
  EU-Horn of Africa Migration Route
    Initiative, 139
  forced migration and, 29–30, 34
  Jordan-EU Compact on
    immigration, 138, 145–146
  Qualification Directive and, 34
  subsidiary protection and, 34
  Temporary Protection Directive and, 35

F

families, 57–61
family separation, 30
federalism, 113–114, 154–155
first "safe country" requirements, 29
forced migration
  agreements with transit countries
    and, 29–30
  annual rates and limits on, 26
  application process for refugee status
    and, 26, 30, 31
  asylum grants and, 25–26
  attempts to limit definition of refugee
    and, 31
  broadening definition of, 32–37
  CAT and, 26
  child separation and, 30
  definition of, 24–26, 31–33
  development of legal status of refugee
    and, 24–27
  distinction between migrants and
    refugees and, 32

EU policies and, 29–30, 34
expedited removal and, 30
family separation, 30
first "safe country" requirements and, 29
Geneva Convention (1951) and, 24–29,
    32–35
geographic insulation and, 28
humanity claims and, 34
human rights and, 24
interdiction and, 29
international agreements, 29
managing and limiting protection
    and, 28–31
nonreturn (nonrefoulement) as
    basic protection of refugee status
    and, 24–26
nonreturn (nonrefoulement) without
    asylum and, 26
Papua New Guinea and Nauru and, 29
politically viable policies and, 27
practical control as basis of political
    differences on, 26–27
protecting under stress and, 27–28
protection as exceptional act of sovereign
    grace and, 27
protection since WWII of, 24–27
questions over numbers of, 27
resettlement in neighboring countries
    of, 28
shunting asylum seekers to Central
    America and, 30
suspicion of, 28
technology permitting increases in, 27
Temporary Protected Status (TPS)
    and, 34–36
US policies and, 25–26, 28–31, 34,
    35–36, 38–39
withholding of removal and, 26
Fourteenth Amendment, 22, 42, 48
Frisch, Max, 79–80

G
Garland, Merrick, 31
gender, 2, 18, 150
Geneva Convention (1951), 24–29, 32–35
geographic insulation, 28
Gentlemen's Agreement (Japan), 44
Germany and immigration, 38, 134
getting in and keeping out

adopted children and, 60
belonging claims and, 58–60, 64–67
COVID-19 and, 62
definition of child and, 58
definition of immediate relatives and, 58
definition of spouse and, 58
discrimination and, 65–67
diversity lottery and, 67
families and, 57–61
H-1B temporary workers and, 63
humanity claims and, 58–60, 64–67
inadmissibility and, 65–66
integration and, 68–69
interim entry permission and, 59–60
investors and, 64–65
limiting entrants and, 65–66
long waits and, 59
Muslim ban and, 65
numbers of immigrants and, 68–69
overview of, 57
per-country limits and, 66–68
same-sex marriage and, 59
siblings and, 60
undocumented immigration
    and, 61–63, 68–69
US policies and, 58, 63, 65–67
workers and, 62–64
Graham v. Richardson (1971), 46–49

H
H-1B category, 63, 70–71
Hawaii, Trump v. (2018), 52–53
historically disadvantaged, 127–130
history's role in immigration policy, 4–5,
    42–45, 156–159
Holocaust, The, 24
Homestead Act (1862), 43–44
humanity claims
    belonging claims and, 9–11
    better responses to forced migration
        and, 36–39
    borders and belonging and, 9–11,
        148–149, 152–156
    child separation and, 19
    definition of, 19
    dignity and, 19
    discretion and, 152–153
    enforcement and, 19, 104, 108–109,
        114, 116

humanity claims (*Continued*)
    family separation and, 19
    forced migration and, 34
    getting in and keeping out and, 58–60,
      64–67
    human rights and, 19
    national borders and, 19–20
    people without lawful status and, 93
    Universal Declaration of Human Rights
      (UDHR) and, 19
human rights, 4, 9, 19, 24, 33, 35, 137, 140,
    142
Hurricane Katrina, 127

I
Immigration Act (1965), 46
Immigration and Customs Enforcement
    (ICE), 107
immigration policy. *See also* better responses
    to forced migration; forced migration;
    getting in and keeping out; people
    without lawful status; temporary
    and indefinite stays; undocumented
    immigration
    all migrants considered in, 38
    belonging claims and, 21
    delegation and, 154–155
    discretion and, 152–155
    fair and accurate results and, 151–152
    goals of, 159–160
    history's role in, 4, 156–159
    making of, 134–135, 151
    overview of, 3–11, 151–156
    realistic and utopian and, 159–160
Immigration Reform and Control Act
    (IRCA), 90, 98
immigration reform of 1965, 44–46,
    66–67, 89, 159
inadmissibility, 65–66
injustices concealed by border, 3, 147–151
insiders, 50–53
integration
    forced migrants and, 38
    getting in and keeping out and, 68–69
    laws and policies that actively
      promote, 22
    national borders and, 21–22
    public commitment to fostering, 22
interdiction, 29–30

interim entry permission, 59–60
international agreements and
    cooperation, 29, 134–135
international trade, 122, 125–126, 134
investors, 64–65
IRCA (Immigration Reform and Control
    Act), 90, 98

J
Jordan-EU Compact on immigration
    (2016), 138, 145–146
Judt, Tony, 159

K
Kennedy, John F., 125
Kerry v. Din (2015), 52
Khartoum Process, 139

L
L-1 category, 71
labor migration, 62–64, 85, 134–135
Landon v. Plasencia (1982), 49–50
lawful migration pathways, 142–143, 145,
    156, 159
limits on immigration numbers, 26, 44,
    68–69

M
Marshall Plan, 141–142
Mediterranean forced migration, 29
methodological approaches, 8–11
Mexican-American War (1848), 45
Mexico-US migration. *See* US immigration
    from Mexico
Miles, Jack, 127
Muñoz, Department of State v.
    (2024), 52–53
Muñoz, Sandra, 52–53
Muslim ban (2017), 52, 65, 66, 149–150

N
NAFTA (North American Free Trade
    Agreement), 134–135
national borders
    belonging claims and, 20–22
    boundaries in other settings and, 16–17
    fairness and justness of, 18
    harms of, 18
    humanity claims and, 19–20
    integration and, 21–22

moving toward better borders and, 18
overview of, 15–16, 22
skepticism about, 15–16
national security concerns, 52, 66, 132
numbers of immigrants, 26, 44, 68–69

O
Obama, Barack
    Arizona Senate Bill 1070 and, 113–114
    DACA and, 73
    enforcement and, 113–114
    financial crisis stimulus response
        and, 125, 130–131
    trade adjustment programs and, 125
outsourcing of border control, 139–141

P
parole, 36, 39, 59–60, 72–73
people without lawful status. See also
        undocumented immigration
    assessing legalization and, 93–95
    asylum as legalization and, 91
    belonging claims and, 90, 94
    Bracero program and, 88–89
    cancellation of removal and, 91
    cap on immigrants from Western
        hemisphere and, 89
    children without lawful status
        and, 93–94
    creation of illegal entry and reentry
        crimes and, 88
    DACA and, 93, 96–97
    Dillingham Commission and, 87
    discretion and, 88–90
    DREAM Act and, 93
    humanity claims and, 93
    immigration reform of 1965 and, 89
    inconclusiveness of US system by design
        and, 96–97
    innocence emphasized for legalization
        and, 93–94
    IRCA and, 90, 98
    labor and race and, 86–90
    lack of clear moral line between
        undocumented and lawful status, 92
    lawful permanent residents and, 91–92
    legalization in context and, 90–93
    limits of legalization and, 97–100

national origins system abolished
        and, 89
    number of undocumented immigrants
        in US and, 89–90
    overview of, 85
    registry and, 91, 99–100
    rule of law and, 95–97
    social cohesion and, 94–95
    Special Immigrant Juvenile Status (SIJS)
        and, 91
    statutes of limitations and, 94–95
    time already lived in country and, 94
    Temporary Protected Status (TPS)
        and, 96–97
    US Citizenship Act (2021) and, 90
    US immigration from Mexico
        and, 87–90
per-country limits, 66–68
Plasencia, Landon v. (1982), 49–50
Plyler v. Doe (1982), 48–49
Postel, Hannah, 136
protection for forced migrants
    approaches to, 32–36
    better responses to forced migration
        and, 32–33
    managing and limiting, 28–31
    narrowness of, 32–33
    stress and, 27–28
public treasury effects, 123–124

Q
Qualification Directive (EU), 34

R
race in immigration history, 42–45,
        86–90. See also civil rights framework;
        discrimination
Reagan, Ronald, 125
realistic and utopian approaches, 8–11,
        116, 159–160
realistic utopia, 8–11, 116, 159–160
Refugee Convention (Organization of
        African Unity) (1969), 32–33
refugees, 24–27
registry, 91, 99–100
religion. See discrimination
remittances, 78, 143–145
Richardson, Graham v. (1971), 46–49
Roosevelt, Theodore, 44

root causes of migration. *See* addressing migration's root causes
rule of law, 49, 95–97

S

same-sex marriage, 58–59
Sandford, Dred Scott v. (1857), 42
Sessions, Jeff, 31
siblings, 58, 60
slavery, 42, 86
social cohesion, 94–95
Social Security, 123–124
Special Immigrant Juvenile Status (SIJS), 91
state and local immigration authority, 113–114, 154–155
Supreme Court (US)
  Brown v. Board of Education (1954), 48
  civil rights framework and, 42, 46–50, 52–53
  Department of State v. Muñoz (2024), 52–53
  Dred Scott v. Sandford (1857), 42
  Graham v. Richardson (1971), 46–49
  Kerry v. Din (2015), 52
  Landon v. Plasencia (1982), 49–50
  Plyler v. Doe (1982), 48–49
  Trump v. Hawaii (2018), 52–53
  undocumented immigration and, 48–49

T

taking skeptics seriously
  African Americans impacted and, 127–130
  Cuban immigrants and, 121
  cultural anxiety and, 131
  deeper anxieties and, 130–132
  discrimination and, 127–130
  economic anxiety and, 124–127
  economic effects and, 120–123
  H1-B category and, 125
  historically disadvantaged and, 127–130
  international trade and, 125–126
  overview of, 119–120
  public treasury effects and, 123–124
  Social Security and, 123–124
  studies of economic impact of immigration and, 121–123

trade adjustment programs and, 125–126
temporary and indefinite stays
  belonging claims and, 81
  choices for migrants and, 79–82
  DACA and, 71, 73–75, 77
  definition of, 70–75
  E-1 and E-2 categories and, 71
  H-1 B category and, 70–71
  in-between status and, 72–75
  L-1 category and, 71
  overview of, 70
  parole and, 72–73
  precarity of in-between status and, 74–75
  problems with, 78–79
  reasons for temporary and in-between and, 75–78
  temporary statuses and, 70–71
  Temporary Protected Status (TPS) and, 71, 73, 74–75, 77
  US policies and, 70–75, 81
Temporary Protected Status (TPS)
  borders and belonging and, 153
  civil rights framework and, 50
  definition of, 34
  designations of, 34
  enactment of, 34
  forced migration and, 34–36
  insiders and, 50
  overview of, 34–36
  people without lawful status and, 96–97
  temporary and indefinite stays and, 71, 73, 74–75, 77
Temporary Protection Directive (EU), 35
trade adjustment programs, 125–126
transit countries, 29–30, 135, 137–141
transparency, 107–108, 114, 116, 140–141, 145–146, 153–155
Treaty of Guadalupe-Hidalgo (1848), 45, 87, 158
Trump, Donald
  attempts to limit definition of refugees under, 31
  Biden's continuation of border policies of, 30–31
  border "crises" and, 54
  COVID-19 and, 30
  enforcement under, 107–109

first "safe country" requirements
and, 29–30
Migrant Protection Protocols
and, 30–31
Muslim ban and, 52, 65, 66, 149–150
shunting asylum seekers to Central
America under, 30
Title 42 and, 30–31
wall and, 109
Trump v. Hawaii (2018), 52–53

U
Ukrainian forced migrants, 38–39
Undesirable Aliens Act (1929), 45
undocumented immigration. *See also*
people without lawful status
borders and belonging and, 156–159
civil rights framework and, 47–49, 51
getting in and keeping out and, 61–63,
68–69
insiders and, 51
numbers of, 47–48
Supreme Court (US) and, 48–49
terminology of, 48
Universal Declaration of Human Rights
(UDHR), 19
US Citizenship Act (2021), 90
US Citizenship and Immigration Services
(USCIS), 107
US immigration from Mexico
addressing migration's root causes
and, 137–138
better responses to forced migration
and, 28–31
borders and belonging and, 158–159
Bracero program and, 47–48, 88, 89,
134
civil rights framework and, 45

enforcement and, 103, 109, 112
people without lawful status and, 87–90
US policies. *See also* Supreme Court (US)
blocking access to protection condition
by, 28–29
borders and belonging and, 151
Bracero program, 47–48, 88, 89, 134
colonialism and, 150
COVID-19 and, 30
enforcement and, 102–104, 107,
114–115
expedited removal and, 30
families in immigration policy and, 58
first "safe country" policy and, 29
gender and, 150
getting in and keeping out and, 58, 63,
65–67
H-1B temporary workers and, 63
interdiction and, 29
labor migration and, 62–64
Migrant Protection Protocols and, 30
refugees and asylum and, 25–26, 28–31,
34, 35–36, 38–39
temporary and indefinite stays
and, 70–75, 81
Temporary Protected Status and, 34–36
Title 42 and, 30
Ukrainian forced migrants and, 38–39
veneer of compliance with Refugee
Convention and, 28–29
work-based immigration and, 62–64

V
Voting Rights Act (1965), 46

W
walls for enforcement, 109
workers and migration, 62–64